The Angels Are Watching

How God Uses Your Life to Teach the Angels

By Aaron D. Taylor

The Angels are Watching
by Aaron D. Taylor

Printed in the United States of America

ISBN 1-59781-478-4

www.xulonpress.com

Table of Contents

Acknowledgments

I would like to thank, first of all, the Holy Spirit for giving me the idea to write this book. I believe that the contents in this little book contain a vital message for the Church in this hour. After reading the first two chapters, it will become obvious to the reader that this is not a book about guardian angels, but a book about life, meaning, significance, value, and the story behind the story that fits everything together. It gives me great joy as a Christian author to be able to expound on the meaning of Scripture and to motivate believers to reevaluate the priorities in their lives.

It would be very dishonest of me, however, to say that the ideas in this book have not been influenced by the teachings and examples of others. I would like to thank Dianne Kannady from Riches in Christ Ministries for faithfully fulfilling her ministry as a teacher in the Body of Christ. Thank you, Dianne, for reviewing the contents of this book and for keeping me grounded in the Scriptures during the formative years of my life and ministry.

I would also like to thank my friend Jack Harris for being a mentor to me in ministry. Thank you, Jack, for all your words of encouragement. Thank you for mentoring me at a time when I had no one else to show me the ropes of the mission field. Your example as an evangelist, pastor, mobilizer, networker, and disciple-maker has proven invaluable in my life. Thank you for believing in me.

To Scott Wood and Eddie Hyatt whose ministries helped to inspire and challenge me while I was in Bible school.

To all the pastors at South County Christian Center, especially Senior Pastor Roy Gerald. Thank you for standing by my wife and me in ministry. We are truly grateful for all the support that you have given us.

To Rick and Donna Shelton, founders of Life Christian Church in St. Louis, the church that I was raised in. Thank you for providing me with a biblical foundation throughout my childhood and teenage years.

To all the churches and individuals that partner with us financially, thank you for standing with us during this time of transition in our lives.

To my parents, Dave and Pam Taylor, thank you for raising me in a godly Christian home. Thank you especially for your love, encouragement, and support. You are an excellent example of what a Christian couple should be.

To Eliot O'Brien, my father-in-law, whose generosity has served as a tremendous inspiration in my life. To Nedra O'Brien who recently, after suffering years with inoperable cancer, went to be with the Lord. It was partially the courageous example of Nedra O'Brien in the midst of her agonizing trial that provided the inspiration for this book.

I would like to thank my wife, Rhiannon, for loving me, taking care of me, and for being my best friend. Rhiannon, we have been through a lot together over the past few years. I know that our love for God and for each other will give us many more beautiful years together.

And, lastly, I would like to thank you, the reader, for taking the time to hear what this young preacher has to say.

Prologue

You are being watched. Every moment. Every second. Even the smallest details of your life are charged with significance. From the valleys to the storms. From the victories to the defeats. Every reaction to every trial is recorded in the books of heaven. Every word spoken out of your mouth is an open screen. Your life is being watched by the angels....and God is teaching them through you. For most of your life you have been unaware. That is...until now. Enter behind the veil.

CHAPTER ONE

World's Darkest Hour

*...who for the joy that was set before Him endured the cross,
despising the shame...*
Hebrews 12:2

Allow me to take you back in time to the world's darkest hour. Not only the world's, but yours and mine as well. Take a look at Jesus as He is hanging on the cross—cold, naked, hungry, thirsty, tortured, humiliated, and, above all, abandoned. Do you see Him? Abandoned by the Father. Abandoned by the world. Abandoned by His friends. What could have possibly been going through His mind?

Flash back. The garden. Adam. Sweet fellowship in the cool of the day. The apple of my eye. Betrayal! Anguish! Come back to me, Adam!

Crack! Another whip tears through His flesh. The crowd spits. The soldiers laugh.

Flash back. The world. The flood. Noah. Deep sorrow over creating mankind. Every thought of man only evil continually. Come back to me, world. I never left you!

Crash! Another soldier's fist lands on His face.

Flash back. The tower of Babel. One people. One language. One unified rebellion.

Thorns piercing through His skull. Another nail crushing through His bones.

I have shown you, O man, what is good; And what does the Lord require of you but to do justly, to love mercy, and to walk humbly with your God? [1]

"If you are the Son of God, come down from the cross. He saved others, let him save himself," shouts the angry crowd.

Oh Jerusalem, Jerusalem, the one who kills the prophets and stones those who are sent to her! How often I wanted to gather your children together, as a hen gathers her chicks under her wings, but you were not willing! [2]

Can you see still see Him? Broken. Tormented. Crushed by the world He created. Do not look away. This is your history and my history. Weep with me as we read the words of the Apostle John together: *"He was in the world, and the world was made through Him, and the world did not know Him."* [3]

Imagine the broken heart of Jesus as He walked the hill of Calvary carrying the cross forced upon Him by the people He came to save. As the *"lamb slain before the foundation of the world,"* [4] He knew that it would eventually come to this. But the people who were mocking and tormenting Him were His creation! It was *He* who sent them rain to water their wells. It was *He* who sent the sun to warm their day. And to make matters worse, these were people created in His image!

Now let's look at the scene from another perspective—*the perspective of the angels.* Since the beginning of human history, the angels were active witnesses of God's peculiar love for this class of being called man. It must have been a strange day for the angels when God created Adam and Eve in His own image, placed them in a beautiful garden, and gave them dominion over all the earth. Probably in their not-too-distant memories was the scene where Satan and his band of rebels were cast out of heaven for daring to assert God-like status for themselves.[5] Now, here is a class of being created in the image of God seemingly for the unique purpose of fellowship. In fact, from God's perspective, He created man a little lower than Himself!

Strangely, when Satan and a third of the angels fell from heaven, there was no hope for restoration.[6] But when man turned his back against God, God came running after him! *Adam, Where are you?* Then, when humanity was at its lowest point, God did the unthinkable. He left heaven and became one of them! Never did He do this for the angels.[7] And now, here is Jesus (a.k.a. God) being nailed to the cross by the very people He loved the most! Given the utter depravity of human history up until the time of the crucifixion, it seemed like God was wasting His love on a worthless band of rebels. *Or was He?*

Now journey back with me to the Garden of Gethsemane. Listen to the Savior's anguish as He sweats with drops of blood. *"Father, if it be possible, let this cup pass from me!"*[8] Sometimes I look back at this scene and wonder, given His state of mind, what could have possibly motivated Jesus to go through what He did? Was it because there was anything in man worth saving? I doubt it. Look at the disciples. Here Jesus is ready to suffer the unimaginable to save their souls and He gives them one simple request: Stay awake and pray. He returns and finds them sleeping. Can you hear His frustration when He says, *"Could you not watch one hour?"*[9] If He was looking for encouragement from His disciples, He was certainly not finding it. In fact, when He needed them the most, what did they do? They forsook Him and fled.[10] And these were His best friends on earth!

Now back to the cross. The insults. The sour wine. The crown of thorns. The spit. The plucking of the beard. His visage was marred more than any man. The hour of darkness had come. *"Father, forgive them, for they know not what they do."* [11]All the legions of hell were unleashed to torture His innocent soul. What held Him on the cross? Love. Did we deserve His love? Hardly. We already know what we get from the cross. Forgiveness of sins. But, after enduring the horrors of the cross inflicted by the very people He created, what could God possibly receive for Himself as a reward for His sacrifice? The answer to this question is where you and I come in.

CHAPTER TWO

Why Am I Here?

Having made known to us the mystery of His will, according to His good pleasure which He purposed in Himself, that in the dispensation of the fullness of the times He might gather together in one all things in Christ, both which are in heaven and which are on the earth – in Him.
Ephesians 1:9-10

Have you ever asked yourself the question, *"Why am I here?"* This is a question that people of all different races, religions, and backgrounds have asked since the beginning of human history. For the atheist, the answer is to eat, breathe, pay taxes, and return to the dirt. For Christians, however, we know that there is a God in heaven and that He created us for a reason. Because of this, Bible believing Christians often ask, *"What is the will of God for my life?"* Although this is a reasonable question, I do not believe that it should be the starting point in discerning the will of God for our lives. After all, how often do we mistake the voice of our own fleshly desires for the voice of the Holy Spirit? A better question to start with is, *"What is God's will for God?"* Once we discover God's will for Himself, we can then discover what His will is for our own lives.

It is in discovering what God wants for Himself that the true meaning of life is found. The purpose of God for our lives revolves around the purpose of God for Himself. In discovering God's will for Himself, we can then peel back the veil of the physical world and discover the true mysteries of the universe.

Here is where the secret lies: It is not about *us* – it is about *Him*. This truth alone is enough to transform the world if mankind could only grasp its implications. In a world filled with suffering, people are grasping for the wind in order to find answers. One major religion, Buddhism, says that the root of all suffering is desire. Therefore, if we can empty ourselves of our desires, we can find an end to suffering by arriving at Nirvana, the ultimate state of nothingness. I disagree. The problem with this view is that it is self-defeating. The reason why a Buddhist empties himself or herself of desires is for the *desire* of a better life of peace and tranquility. This view fails to recognize that desire is inevitable.

The root of human misery is not desire, but *misplaced* desire. If I find my satisfaction in life from pursuing my *own* happiness, then I will ultimately end up miserable and disappointed because there are too many things in life that could make me unhappy. *Death. Disease. Pain. Rejection. Failure.* The reason why the pursuit of pleasure never leads to satisfaction is because too many things in life are *unpleasant*. As the Apostle Paul says, *"She who lives in pleasure is dead while she lives."*[12] Those who live for pleasure will always end up with the short end of the stick. King Solomon had all the earthly pleasures that a man could ask for. *Wealth. Power. Glory.* And yet, at the end of his life, he came to the conclusion that *"all is vanity and grasping for the wind."* [13]

If I can, however, find my satisfaction in life from pursuing not my *own* pleasure, but the pleasure of *another*, then I can take *all* that life throws my way—the good, the bad, and the ugly—and channel it for a higher purpose. But, even in this, I must be careful. I must determine *who* it is that I am living for. If I live for the pleasure of other people, I will still end up miserable and disappointed because people by nature are very difficult to please. Even the noblest of intentions displayed in the greatest of charity to the greatest of human suffering will ultimately lead to disappointment because the people I seek to serve and please will always ask for more than I can give. If I live for the happiness of others, then I myself will be unhappy when they are unhappy with me. By seeking to please the miserable, I myself become miserable. Therefore, the only option I have left to find true satisfaction in life is to live for someone who loves me unconditionally and is infinitely greater than myself. After studying all the major religions and philosophies of the world, I have found that the only someone worthy of this type of devotion is the God of the Bible revealed in Jesus Christ. It is only in serving the God of the Bible revealed in the person of Jesus Christ that one can honestly say, *"We love Him because he first loved us."*[14]

Herein lies the beauty of Christianity. We serve a God that is infinitely worthy to be served. We do not serve a God who is so high up in the heavens that He cannot relate to human frailty. The God of the Bible has shown us what love is by wrapping Himself in human flesh and suffering with us. The Bible says, *"We do not have a High Priest who cannot sympathize with our weaknesses."*[15] When Jesus was suffering on the cross, God was saying to all of humanity, *"Come back to me. The way is open. I love you. I accept you. I want to help you."* Even in the midst of our rebellion, Christ died for us. The Bible says, *"But God demonstrates His own love toward us in that, while we were still sinners, Christ died for us."* [16]

It is in accepting and receiving this unconditional love that we are able to give the same love away to others. Jesus said *"This is my commandment that you love one another as I have loved you."* [17] Often, I have heard it said that the golden rule is to treat others the way you want to be treated. Although this is certainly true, I believe that the truth actually goes much deeper than this. For the Christian, the golden rule is to treat others the way that *God* has treated *us*. The Apostle John puts it very simply when He says, *"Beloved, if God so loved us, we also ought to love one another."* [18]

Not only does the cross of Christ provide us with the basis for serving others; it also destroys the basis for serving God for selfish reasons. If I serve God and obey His commandments only to save myself from eternal punishment, then I am ultimately serving God for a selfish reason—namely, to save myself. This is what man-made religion teaches. Obey the rules and save yourself. The problem with this view is that it leads to self-righteousness. This is why the Jewish leaders rejected Jesus. They did not want to hear that their meticulous efforts to follow the law of God perfectly did nothing to earn a place for them in the kingdom of heaven. The Apostle Paul has this to say about the Jewish leaders who rejected Jesus: *"But Israel, pursuing the law of righteousness, has not attained to the law of righteousness. Why? Because they did not seek it by faith, but as it were, by the works of the law. For they stumbled at the stumbling stone."*[19]

If I can earn my place in heaven by being a good person, then ultimately I *deserve* my place in heaven. But the Bible says, *"If righteousness comes through the law, then Christ died in vain."*[20] Christianity begins with the fact that *"all have sinned and fallen short of the glory of God"*[21] and therefore, there is nothing that man can do to save himself from the wrath of a holy and righteous God. Trying to live a good life in order to earn a place in heaven is to serve God for selfish reasons and leads to self-righteousness. The suffering of Christ on the cross destroys the basis for this faulty assumption.

Not only does the cross of Christ destroy the basis for our self-righteousness, it also morally obligates us to serve Him by following His commandments. It is this sense of moral obligation to follow Jesus in light of His suffering on the cross that constitutes genuine repentance. Without this repentance, there is no true salvation. This is why Christ died on the cross, so that He could establish His rightful place as Lord of our lives. The Bible says, *"For to this end Christ died and rose and lived again, that He might be Lord of both the dead and the living."* [22]

Think about it for a moment. Christ died on the cross so that He could establish His place as the rightful sovereign over human hearts. This is the God-side of redemption. Often, we as Christians tend to think of our salvation in terms of "what do *I* get out of it?" But have you ever stopped and asked yourself, "What does *God* get from my salvation?" When we discover the answer to this question, we will discover the answer to our original question: *What is God's will for God?* The answer may surprise you.

Let's look at Ephesians 4:9-10 for a clue to this mystery.

Now this, 'He ascended'—what does it mean but that He also first descended into the lower parts of the earth? He who descended is also the One who ascended far above all the heavens, that He might fill all things.

The Bible is saying here that Christ died and rose again so that He might fill all things. You may be saying to yourself, *"What? I thought that Christ died on the cross so that I don't have to go to hell."* That is only part of it. There is a higher purpose for why Christ died for you. Let's look at another clue found in Ephesians 1:9-10.

Having made known to us the mystery of His will, according to His good pleasure which He purposed in Himself, that in the dispensation of the fullness of the times He might gather together in one all things in Christ, both which are in heaven and which are on earth – in Him.

Philosophers and sages searching for the meaning of life need search no further. The great secret behind the universe is that everything exists for Christ. It is not about us. It is about Him. He is the beginning and the end—the goal of all things. According to this passage of Scripture, one day all of creation will find its ultimate fulfillment in Christ.

Why did Jesus die and rise again? *So that He might fill all things.* The ultimate goal of the cross was not merely to redeem mankind. Redeeming mankind is what *we* get out of it. The ultimate goal of the cross is God the Father bringing glory to God the Son. Think about what Jesus said shortly before going to the cross: *"The hour has come that the Son of Man should be glorified."* [23] What a strange thing to say! Torture and starvation and humiliation hardly sound like glorification to me. *Was Jesus crazy?* No, He was not. Here is why.

Before time began, God the Father had a desire to glorify God the Son. This is why God created the universe and everything in it, including the invisible angelic realm. Here is what the Bible has to say about Christ (God the Son):

For By Him all things were created that are in heaven and that are on the earth, visible and invisible, whether thrones or dominions or principalities or powers. All things were created through Him and for Him.[24]

Notice it says that all things were created through Him and *for* Him. Christ is literally the reason for everything! God the Father was so pleased with God the Son (Christ) that He created the universe as a means by which He could radiate His splendor. When God created the angels, His intention was for them to worship and serve Christ.[25] Since the universe was created through Christ, the natural response for the angels would be to behold the beauty of creation and to respond by worshiping Him. This would be God the Father's way of bringing glory and honor to God the Son.

All was going well until one day Satan decided that He wanted the glory to go to himself instead of going to Christ. [26] Satan then led a rebellion against God and took a portion of the angels with him.[27] It seemed that the Father's plan had failed. The Son was not receiving the glory that He deserved. How would God the Father take back the glory due His Son? The answer was to create a being capable of reflecting the image of Christ. This is where you and I come in.

When God selected Adam and Eve to represent the human race, He gave them a mandate to *"be fruitful and multiply; fill the earth and subdue it; have dominion over the fish of the sea, over the birds of the air, and over every living thing that moves on the earth."* [28] Because Adam and Eve were created *"in the image of God,"* [29] they were to reflect the glory of Christ to the entire angelic realm. [30] This is why God gave them the mandate to *"fill the earth and subdue it."* To fill the earth is to cover it with the glory of Christ. This is the Father's way of glorifying the Son in the presence of the angels.

Notice the similarity between Genesis 1:28 and Ephesians 4:10. God's mandate to mankind is to *"be fruitful and multiply. Fill the earth and subdue it."* Christ died and rose again *"so that He might fill all things."* Why the similarity? Because God's mandate to mankind and God's fulfillment in Christ are for the same purpose. The ultimate intention of God the Father is to bring glory to Christ.

As man radiates the glory of Christ, the Father's purpose of bringing glory to the Son is fulfilled. Christ died and rose again to make this possible. As men and women become *"new creations in Christ,"* [31] God can then display them as chief objects of His grace to the *"principalities and powers in the heavenly places."*[32] Here is what the Apostle Paul has to say on this matter.

> *And to make all see what is the fellowship of the mystery which from the beginning of the ages has been hidden in God who created all things through Jesus Christ; to the intent that now the manifold wisdom of God might be made known by the Church to the principalities and powers in the heavenly places, according to the eternal purpose which He accomplished in Christ Jesus our Lord.* [33]

God the Father, who *"created all things through Jesus Christ,"* [34] wants to display the Church before the angels! This is His *"eternal purpose which He accomplished through Christ Jesus."*

Now we are closer to answering the question, *What is God's will for God?* We have discovered that the will of God is to bring glory to Christ. God wants to *"gather together in one all things in Christ, both which are in heaven and which are on earth—in Him."* [35] This speaks of the entire created order finding its ultimate fulfillment in Christ. This is God the Father bringing glory to God the Son. [36]

God the Father is so pleased with God the Son that He desires to give Him glory not only through the creation, but through the *redemption* of creation as well. The theme of glory through redemption is beautifully described for us in Colossians 1:19-20:

> *For it pleased the Father that in Him all the fullness should dwell, and by Him to reconcile all things to Himself, by Him, whether things on earth or things in heaven, having made peace through the blood of His cross.*

How awesome it is that God has redeemed the entire created order through the blood of Jesus on the cross! This is God the Father bringing glory to God the Son. The universal value of His sacrifice shows the infinite value of His person.[37] No one single person could have made up this story. It is too contrary to the human way of thinking. *Glory through humiliation? That is foolish!* It is precisely the *"foolishness"* of this message that separates the proud from the humble. Listen with your heart what the Bible has to say on this matter.

> *For the message of the cross is foolishness to those who are perishing, but to us who are being saved it is the power of God. For it is written: 'I will destroy the wisdom of the wise, and bring to nothing the understanding of the prudent.' Where is the wise? Where is the scribe? Where is the disputer of this age? Has God not made foolish the wisdom of this world? For since, in the wisdom of God, the world through wisdom did not know God, it pleased God through the foolishness of the message preached to save those who believe.* [38]

It is through the *"foolishness"* of the cross that God confounds the wise and gives glory to the Son.

As awesome as this truth is, have we gone far enough? No. There is still more to the mystery. Let's dig a little deeper. The final piece of the puzzle is found in I Corinthians 15:24:

> *Then comes the end, when He delivers the kingdom to God the Father, when He puts an end to all rule and all authority and power.*

Just as the Father desires to bring glory to the Son, so the Son desires to give glory back to the Father. This is the great love circle that existed before time began. The great truth of Christianity is that behind all of reality is a relationship. As the Father glorifies the Son through the cross, so the Son gives glory back to the Father through the life of the Church.

This is the story *behind* the story that connects *everything* together. The Father gives glory to the Son. The Son gives glory back to the Father. This is God's will for God. Mysteriously, all of this is accomplished by the power of the Holy Spirit. The great secret behind the universe is that everything exists because of the triune relationship that existed in God before time and space began. Before there ever was an *it*, there existed three eternal *who's* within the one being of God in an eternal relationship of mutual love and harmony. [39]

The desire of God is for the Church to be a reflection of the triune relationship that exists within Himself. Through uniting together people of all different nations, tribes, tongues, and cultures, God brings glory to Himself by bringing unity out of diversity. This, in essence, is the heart of the Great Commission. The original Great Commission did not start with *"Go ye into all the world and preach the gospel."*[40] It actually started with *"Be fruitful and multiply. Fill the earth and subdue it."*[41] Jesus did not actually *give* the Great Commission. He simply *reviewed* it.

When Adam and Eve's descendants failed to take the mandate of God seriously to fill the earth with His glory, God intervened by creating distinct ethnic groups and scattering them throughout the world. This is what took place at the tower of Babel.[42] When the earth became populated, people once again fell into gross idolatry and wickedness. [43] It seems that God was stacking the odds against Himself. The greater the odds, the greater the glory. Since every people group spoke a different language and had their own culture and customs, God now had to reveal Himself to one group of people who would then spread the true knowledge of Him to every other people. This task was given to Abraham and his descendants in Genesis 12:1-3:

> *Now the Lord said to Abraham: "Get out of your country, From your family and from your father's house, to a land that I will show you. I will make you a great nation. I will bless you and make your name great. And you shall be a blessing. I will bless those who bless you, and I will curse him who curses you. And in you all the families of the earth shall be blessed.*

Here we have the most startling declaration in the entire ancient world. This is far from some petty tribal god declaring superiority over all the other tribal gods in the ancient world. This would have been quite common in the polytheistic society of ancient Mesopotamia. Here we have the one true God choosing a man and his descendants to bless every other tribe on the earth. Unthinkable in the ancient world!

The rest of the Bible is the story of God fulfilling His promise to Abraham that in him all the nations of the earth would be blessed. Even though Abraham's immediate descendants failed in their mandate to spread the knowledge of God to every people (as recorded in the Old Testament), amazingly, it was precisely their failure that brought salvation to the Gentiles! [44] Now all who place their faith in Jesus Christ, whether Jew or Gentile, share in both the blessing and responsibility of Abraham. [45] God has reconciled both Jew and Gentile into one body through the cross.[46] This new body of redeemed Jews and Gentiles is what the Bible calls "the Church." It is to the Church that God has passed along the mandate, in connection to His promise to Abraham, to bless every nation of the earth. [47] It is the cross-cultural aspect of the Great Commission that gives God the greatest glory by bringing the greatest unity out of the greatest diversity. It seems that the angels have a front row seat to this drama of the Church fulfilling its mandate given by God Himself. [48]

Will the Church succeed in its mandate? If we fast- forward to the book of Revelation, we get a glimpse of the answer to this question. Here is a song that will be sung in heaven one day in the near future.

> *And they sang a new song, saying: You are worthy to take the scroll, and to open its seals. For you were slain, and have redeemed us to God by your blood out of every tribe and tongue and people and nation, and have made us kings and priests to our God. And we shall reign on the earth.* [49]

All of history is heading to one ultimate climax of every tribe, tongue, people, and nation worshiping at the feet of Jesus. This is God the Father bringing glory to God the Son by bringing unity out of diversity. When it is all said and done, Jesus amazingly delivers the kingdom right back to the Father. [50] It is the great love match of the ages. Here is a vision worth living and dying for. This is God's will for God. Instead of asking, *What is God's will for my life?* we should be asking, *Where does my life fit in to God's will for Himself?* Those who devote their lives to bringing every nation, tribe, and tongue to worship at the feet of Jesus are sure to hit the target.

CHAPTER 3

Teaching Angels

And to make all see what is the fellowship of the mystery, which from the beginning has been hidden in God who created all things through Jesus Christ.

To the intent that now the manifold wisdom of God might be made known by the Church to the principalities and powers in the heavenly places, according to the eternal purpose which He accomplished in Christ Jesus our Lord.
Ephesians 3:10-11

The secret is out. Everything in life has a purpose. And the purpose is about God—not us. When I was a little boy, my mother used to say to me "Aaron, the whole world does not revolve around you." I can remember hearing this over and over as a child. It always got on my nerves when my mother would say this, but I probably needed to hear it. Somehow, I think that we all need to be reminded of this simple truth from time to time. We tend to think that we are the center of the universe. A problem or situation arises in our lives and suddenly we think that God has not kept His Word to us. As if God somehow falls off the throne when things don't go our way!

But the truth of the matter is this—we are created for *Him*, not the other way around. God does not exist to serve us. We exist to serve *Him*. As the Westminster Catechism states, "Man's chief end is to glorify God and enjoy Him forever." We exist solely to give pleasure to God. Period. Nothing else matters.

God is the center of everything that is. The Bible says, *"For of Him and through Him and to Him are all things, to whom be glory forever. "* [51] The sum purpose of all that exists is to give glory back to God. And make no mistake about it, God is passionate about His glory. Listen to what God says to Moses as Moses pleads with Him to spare the people of Israel. *"I have pardoned according to your word, but, truly, as I live, all the earth shall be filled with the glory of the Lord."* [52] Again, hear what God says through the prophet Habakkuk, *"For the earth will be filled with the knowledge of the glory of the Lord, as the waters cover the sea."* [53]

God's chief passion is His own glory. This is why He created us—to display His glory to the rest of His creation. And according to Ephesians 3:10, this includes the angels. In fact, according to this passage, this is why God created the Church. Notice that the verse says, *"To the intent that now the manifold wisdom of God might be made known by the Church to the principalities and powers in the heavenly places."* The purpose of God for the Church is to teach the angels something about His character.

But doesn't it sound a little strange to say that a believer should live his or her life with the consciousness of being watched by angels? To the modern person living in North America or Europe, this may sound a little strange, but to the Apostle Paul and the early Church, it was a living reality that helped define their character.

Consider this verse in I Corinthians 11:10, *"For this reason the woman ought to have a symbol of authority on her head, because of the angels."* Here in this passage, Paul is dealing with women in the church who were flaunting their liberty in Christ by embarrassing their husbands in the public assembly. Apparently, the gospel had so elevated the status of women in Corinthian society that the women in the church felt they could throw modesty out the window. It is likely that the women felt this way because Paul was a radical proponent of equality between the sexes. Although this statement might sound shocking to those who have preconceived ideas about Paul's views on women, remember that it was Paul who taught that *"in Christ there is no male and female."* [53] Furthermore, Paul also taught that, in marriage, husbands and wives have equal responsibility and equal authority in matters relating to child rearing and sexual relations. This was an extremely radical concept during this time period. [54] However, as it still is today, people tend to have selective hearing. The women in the Corinthian church took Paul's teachings on liberty and equality to mean that they could defy their husbands in public by dressing like prostitutes. Paul's point in this verse is that by doing this, the women are not only embarrassing their husbands, they are also making fools of themselves in front of the angels. In essence, they were nullifying one of the primary purposes of the Church, which is *"to make known the wisdom of God to the principalities and powers in the heavenly places."*

Knowing that our lives are meant to reveal the character of God to the angels helps to put our everyday actions into proper perspective. As was the case with the Corinthian women, so is the case with our lives today. Wives, when you disrespect your husbands in public by dressing inappropriately or by cutting him down, remember that you are being watched. Although you may feel that you are only getting even with him for being insensitive or failing to take out the trash, what you are actually doing is making a fool of yourself in front of God's holy angels. The same is true for husbands. So many men love to talk bad about their wives in front of other men so that they can make themselves look macho and feed their own egos. Little do they know that their actions make a mockery of the cross by failing to give God the vindication He deserves for His sacrifice on the cross.

Another verse that indicates the Apostle Paul was aware that his life was on display for the angels is found in I Corinthians 4:9. Here Paul says, *"For I think that God has displayed us, the apostles, last, as men condemned to death; for we have been made a spectacle to the world, both to angels and to men."* The imagery here is of a Roman gladiator fighting for his life before a stadium full of blood-thirsty spectators. Often, at the end of a sporting event in the Roman coliseums, prisoners would be thrown before hungry lions as the crowds watched and cheered. In talking about his sufferings through persecutions, Paul saw himself put on display in a similar way before men and angels. Since it is unlikely that God's holy angels would take sadistic pleasure in the sufferings of Paul, the reference here is probably to fallen angels. If this is the case, then there is more to this verse than what meets the eye.

Paul seems to be saying here that his sufferings are a direct result of fallen angels who would stir the crowds to buffet him and then watch to gloat over their victory. This would explain the reference in II Corinthians 12:7 to Paul's thorn as *"a messenger of Satan sent to buffet me."* The word "messenger" in the Greek is the word *angelos*, which is where we get the word "angel." This word is always used in reference to a spiritual being. In this case, Paul's thorn is a spiritual being (a.k.a. fallen angel) sent from Satan to follow Paul around and stir up the angry crowds to buffet his physical body.

So when Paul says that he is made a *"spectacle to men and angels,"* he is in a way identifying with the sufferings of Christ. Remember that it was Satan and his fallen angels that stirred the crowds to crucify Jesus. [55] As Jesus hung on the cross; He was on display both before the angry crowds and before the fallen angels who stirred them to action. As Paul is put on display before *"men and angels,"* God is vindicated in the highest manner because Paul, as a man in whom dwells the Spirit of Christ, is willing to undergo the same types of sufferings that Christ suffered in order to advance the gospel. How we need more Pauls in this world that will live for the sole purpose of the glory of God and the advance of the gospel! It is this kind of passion and dedication that gives God the greatest amount of glory, honor, and vindication as a reward for His sufferings on the cross. Such was the passion that drove a 16th century group of Christians called the Moravians. This zealous band of Christians took the gospel far beyond the confines of Western Europe. Some even sold themselves into slavery in order to evangelize the North American Indians. Their motto was "to win for the Lamb the reward for His sacrifice."

This ties in to the idea presented in Ephesians 3:10. Notice that the Apostle Paul says the Church is to *"make known the manifold wisdom of God to the principalities and powers in the heavenly places."* If we cross-reference this verse with Ephesians 6:12, we see that the words *"principalities and powers"* are used to describe fallen angels, not God's holy angels (although, in this case, the meaning could be both). How is it that God intends to use our lives to make known His manifold wisdom to fallen angels? The answer lies in the battle for the souls of men. Paul says, *"For we do not wrestle against flesh and blood, but against principalities, against powers, against the rulers of the darkness of this age, against spiritual hosts of wickedness in heavenly places."* [56]

To Paul, the Christian life is a wrestling match against Satan and his band of fallen angels. The prize is the souls of men. As Christians engage in combat against spiritual wickedness in the heavenly places in order to advance the gospel, the manifold wisdom of God is displayed to the very spiritual powers that sought to crucify the Lord Jesus Christ. When Satan and his evil angels crucified Jesus, little did they know that through His death and resurrection God would raise up an entire army of believers bearing the image of Christ who would continue His mission to *"set at liberty those who are oppressed."* [57]

If only the majority of God's people would rise up and join the battle! Too often Western Christians have a cruise ship mentality of the Christian life. To many, salvation is viewed like stepping onto a cruise ship. Rescued from the imminent doom of the raging sea, the believer finds himself or herself on a luxury cruise liner filled with delights and benefits never enjoyed before in his or her life of sin. The remainder of the Christian life is spent exploring the different benefits available on this ship of luxury. To these Christians, spiritual warfare is perceived as simply resisting the devil in order to possess what is rightfully theirs, namely healing, deliverance, and prosperity along with other benefits. While it is true that God wants believers to possess their rights in Christ, defining spiritual warfare this way trivializes its true meaning. True spiritual warfare in the Pauline sense is the struggle for the advance of the gospel.

Often the analogy is given of Christians crossing the Jordan in order to possess the Promised Land. In this view, driving out the Canaanites is likened to driving out the enemies in our lives that keep us from possessing all that God has purchased for us in our redemption. This is the cruise ship mentality. The problem with this idea is that it puts the focus on self and not on the lost. It is this mindset that makes some people think that if they can claim material prosperity for themselves, then somehow that will make the gospel attractive to the lost and drive people into the kingdom. People who think this way need a reality check! The world is not impressed with white picket fences and fancy cars. They don't care if we claim new Cadillacs for ourselves using some newly discovered faith formula. They don't even care when we claim the gospel has lifted us out of poverty and failure into healthy and productive lives. To tell the truth, self-help books can do the same thing. These things are not wrong in and of themselves, but they do not impress unbelievers. What drives unbelievers to their knees is when they see a Christian driven to self-sacrifice by a radical commitment to the gospel.

Paul says of himself, *"Therefore I take pleasure in infirmities, in reproaches, in needs, in persecutions, in distresses, for Christ's sake. For when I am weak, then I am strong."* [58] Notice how Paul says, *"I take pleasure in needs."* What a far cry this is from the consumer gospel so prevalent in American churches today! So often Christians are told that if they were truly following the ways of the Lord, they wouldn't have any needs. They are told that lack is a sign of spiritual failure while abundance is a sign of spiritual success. Even further, they are told that non-believers must see Christians prospering materially in order to make the gospel attractive. I wonder if these same people would dare preach this message to the Apostle Paul who often suffered *hunger and thirst, was poorly clothed, beaten and homeless!* [59] The problem with this idea is that it turns selfishness into a virtue. Although it is true that the will of God *in general* is that believers are to have their needs met and to have *"an abundance for every good work,"*[60] this does not mean that life is intended to be a bed of roses for the believer. Where are the believers today who live lives of such sacrifice and commitment that they gladly take pleasure *in their needs* in order to advance the gospel? Unfortunately, I am sad to say that few can be found in the American Church today.

A more appropriate mentality of the Christian life is not of a cruise ship, but of a battleship. Paul says, *"We wrestle not against flesh and blood."* Jesus did not die on the cross so that Christians could spend their lives "claiming the Promised Land" of self-satisfaction. He died and rose again so that He could raise up a new breed of humanity who would give their lives to fulfill His vision of *"delivering all those who are oppressed of the Devil."* [61] We need to face reality. Hell is real and only the preaching of the cross will save sinners from going there for all eternity. It is when we join the battle for the souls of men that we truly fulfill the vision in the heart of Jesus to *display the wisdom of God before the principalities and powers in the heavenly places.* The battle is real. The stakes are eternal. The angels are watching. How will you respond?

CHAPTER FOUR

Ultimate Value

Of this salvation the prophets have inquired and searched carefully, who prophesied of the grace that would come to you, searching what, or what manner of time, the Spirit of Christ who was in them was indicating when He testified beforehand the sufferings of Christ and the glories that would follow. To them it was revealed that, not to themselves, but to us they were ministering the things which now have been reported to you through those who have preached the gospel to you by the Holy Spirit sent from heaven— **things which angels desired to look into.**

I Peter 1:10-12 (author's emphasis)

You are God's work of art. Although it may seem like your life is insignificant, if you can look behind the veil, you will see that your life is a demonstration to the angels of the wonders of the grace of God. This grace is something that the ancient prophets could only dream about. It is something that angels have desired to look into as far back as the beginnings of human history. It is the image of God stamped in the heart of man. Here is where your ultimate value lies, not in who *you* are, but in who *He* is in you.

Throughout my life, I have always desired strongly to be greatly used by God. I believe that anyone, regardless of their circumstances, who dreams big and acts on their faith can accomplish extraordinary things for the Lord. Through faith, I have traveled the world preaching the gospel, praying for the sick, ministering to leaders, and taking Christian materials into closed countries. Like every other Christian evangelist who has gone on before me, I have had my fair share of disappointment and discouragement. More times than I can count, during my deepest moments of discouragement, I have prayed prayers like *"God, either let me win the world or take me home to be with you."* It is in times like these that the Holy Spirit gently reminds me that my ultimate value lies far more in *being* and far less in *doing*.

So often we in the West think that our value in life depends on what we accomplish. In most Eastern cultures, however, the thinking is different. One's value in life depends on birth and position in Eastern cultures. Both views miss the mark. The real source of value for the believer's life is Christ and Christ alone. The Bible says *"For in Him dwells all the fullness of the Godhead bodily, and you are complete in Him..."* [62] Our true value lies in who *Christ* is, not in who *we* are.

When you are born again, the image of God is imparted to your spirit through the Lord Jesus Christ. [63] This is what makes you valuable regardless of the circumstances you find yourself in. Perhaps you find yourself in a broken marriage. Or perhaps trials and tribulations have ravaged your life and left you broken and destitute. Take heart, my friend. The fact that Christ lives in you means that your life is worth far more than any pearl or precious stone. God sees *Himself* in you. This is why your life is worth far more than what you could ever accomplish in life.

This does not mean, however, that the way a believer lives his or her life is insignificant. The Bible says, *"Christ in you is the hope of glory."* [64] I have heard it said many times from well-intentioned preachers that God does not want to share His glory with man. On one level this is true. God never wants His people to bask in self-exaltation. But on the other hand, nothing can be further from the truth. The Bible says that God *"chose you for salvation through sanctification by the Spirit and belief in the truth, to which He called you by our gospel, for the obtaining of the glory of our Lord Jesus Christ."* [65] This is why God called you into His family, *so that you can obtain the glory of Jesus Christ.* Too often this truth is lost by well-intentioned ministers who fear that exalting man is equal to demoting Christ. This, however, does not change the fact that God's ultimate goal for the believer is *glorification.* As Paul says in Romans 8:29, *"Moreover, whom He predestined, these He also called; whom He called, these he also justified; and whom He justified, these He also glorified."*

It is precisely this glory that God gives to the Church that He wants to display to the myriad of angels in the heavenly realms. It is the process of glorification in the lives of believers that the angels are so intently watching. This is why the purpose of God for the Church is so unique. We, as members of the Body of Christ, because Christ Himself, who is the hope of glory, lives in us, have access to grace that previously was unavailable to men and women for thousands of years before the Church came into existence.

Now we can understand what the Apostle Peter is saying when He says, *"of this salvation, the prophets have inquired and searched carefully, who prophesied of the grace that would come to you."* [66] The grace available to believers today is far superior to anything experienced by even the greatest prophets in the Old Testament. This is why Jesus could say that *He who is the least in the Kingdom of Heaven is greater than John the Baptist.* [67] For thousands of years after the sin of Adam and Eve, man had been banished from the measure of the grace of God that would have enabled them to live Christ-like lives. Although they could experience the grace of God in part, they did not have access to the resurrection power of Jesus simply because Jesus had not yet gone to the cross and risen from the dead. When Jesus rose from the dead, He became a *"life-giving Spirit"* [68] able to impart the life of God into the spirits of men and women. It is this life that recreates the human spirit and puts him into a new class of being. This is what the Apostle Paul means when He says, *"If any man be in Christ, he is a new creation. Old things have passed away, behold, all things become new."* [69] Why did God wait for thousands of years to make this grace available to mankind? We may never know for sure. But one thing we can be sure of is that it was not for our own glory, but for *His* glory. As the Apostle Peter reminds us, these are *"things which angels desired to look into."* [70]

Brothers and sisters in Christ, how awesome it is to know that we are a demonstration of the grace of God to innumerable hosts of angels in the heavenly realms! Because Christ lives in us, we are a demonstration of the nature and character of God not only to the world around us, but to the invisible world as well. This is why every moment of the Christian life is significant. Our everyday actions count more than we realize. Just as God demonstrated His love for us by becoming a man and dying on the cross to bear the punishment for our sins, so we demonstrate our love for God by vindicating Him before the angelic realm by our words and actions.

Remember that when Satan and his band of rebellious angels fell, God offered no hope for redemption. But when man fell from his original state of glory, God did the unthinkable. God, in the person of Jesus Christ, left heaven and took on the nature of a man, subjected Himself to the cruelty of the cross (at the hands of man) for the sole purpose of rising again. The goal of His death and resurrection was so that He could give man a new nature. Many Christians do not realize that the death of Christ was not an end in itself; it was merely a means to an end. It is through the death of Christ that God puts to death our old sinful nature,[71] but it is through the resurrection of Christ that God imparts His life and nature into us and raises us to a new life in Him. [72] Christ died *so that* He could be raised up. And Christ was raised up so that He could create a new man in His image with His character and holiness. [73] God never did anything remotely close to this for the angels who fell from heaven. Perhaps this is why angels are so baffled at God's unique love for man. Perhaps this is why our salvation is something that *"angels desired to look into."* For whatever reason God chose to do it this way, one thing we know for sure is that God intends to use the lives of believers to demonstrate His glory to the angels.

Having this perspective helps to put the trials and struggles in our lives into proper focus. I have often wondered about the *"count it all joy"* passages in the Bible that tell us that we should rejoice when we fall into various testings and trials. [74] On a purely natural level, it seems utterly absurd to rejoice when all hell breaks loose in our lives. But when we realize that the ultimate purpose of our lives is to give glory to God, we are free to rejoice because trials give us an opportunity to give unto God the glory He deserves. What better way to give glory to God than to praise Him in the midst of turmoil and hardship? As David says, *"I will bless the Lord at all times, His praise shall continually be in my mouth."* [75] It is only when our sole satisfaction in life comes from giving glory to God that we can say that we have truly died to self. And it is only when we die to self that we are truly free to live. Jesus said, *"If anyone desires to come after Me, let him deny himself, take up his cross and follow Me."* [76] As we die to our own rights, we find true freedom in Christ. And as we live out our freedom in Christ (that is, freedom from self), we demonstrate the glory of God before men and angels and thus fulfill our ultimate purpose.

Consider the story of Job for example. The story of Job is an excellent example of how God can use the life of one dedicated person to demonstrate His glory to the angels. Job was a man who had everything that life could offer in the ancient world: riches, fame, power, good health and a large family. Apparently, Job's life was being watched intently in the heavenly realms. To Satan and his fallen angels, it was painstakingly obvious to their evil hearts that God was responsible for the abundance of prosperity for Job and his family. When Satan, along with his fallen angels, approached God regarding Job, they accused Job of serving God solely because of the blessings that He had provided for him. It is important to understand that this was not only an accusation against Job, but an accusation against God for showering His abundant kindness on someone that Satan and his fallen angels felt was unworthy. Satan said to God, *"Have you not made a hedge around him, around his household, and around all that he has on every side? You have blessed the work of his hands, and his possessions have increased in the land. But now, stretch out Your hand and touch all that he has, and he will surely curse you to your face!"* [77]

Satan's accusation against God is not unlike the accusation that many people throughout history have made against God as well. *God, why have you blessed that person and not me?* The problem with this accusation is that it assumes that God owes us something. The truth is that God owes us nothing. We owe *Him* for our very existence. The Bible teaches that God can have mercy and compassion on whomever He chooses. It appears that, in calling Satan's bluff, God was teaching the angels (and us all) a lesson about His character. No one has a right to accuse God regarding the distributions of His blessings.

It seemed that the life of Job was headed for unbridled bliss. That is, until one day when tragedy struck and Job lost everything. Although Job was a righteous man, his faith was put to a severe test through his tragic loss of family and possessions. Not only did he lose everything he owned, he also suffered a severe physical affliction that brought him great pain and turmoil. The response of most people would be to curse God and die. In fact, Job's wife suggested that he do this very thing. But what was Job's response? *"The Lord gave and the Lord has taken away. Blessed be the name of the Lord."* [78]

What a shock this must have been to Satan and his band of fallen angels who came to present themselves before the Lord for the sole purpose of challenging Job's integrity! Often it is emphasized how Job was vindicated in this story. Although this is true, there is a message that actually goes deeper than this. In a similar way that God desires to use the Church to *"make known His manifold wisdom to the principalities and powers in the heavenly places,"* God used the life of Job to demonstrate His glory to Satan and his fallen angels. Not only is Job vindicated in this story, *God* is vindicated in this story.

Although I have emphasized the lasting significance of Job's sufferings, I would like to make it clear at this point that I am *not* saying that God purposefully inflicts pain and suffering on His servants so that He can bring glory to Himself. To draw this conclusion is to misread the material. Many people use the book of Job to try to find an explanation for why God allows the righteous to suffer. The problem with this is that it misses the point of the entire story. When Job tries to get an answer from God as to the reason behind his sufferings, God never answers Him. Instead, He asks Job a series of questions to show him the greatness of His sovereignty. [79] Every time in the Bible when someone asks God why He allows the righteous to suffer, they are never given an answer. Apparently, this is something that God does not intend for us to know. This is why it is wrong to read the book of Job and to try to figure out who was responsible for Job's sufferings. Was it God? Was it Satan? Or was it Job? The answer is that it really doesn't matter. The Bible says *"The secret things belong to the Lord our God, those things which are revealed belong to us."* [80]

Let's look at what the New Testament has to say about how we should interpret the story of Job. The Apostle James has this to say:

My brethren, take the prophets who spoke in the name of the Lord as an example of suffering and patience. Indeed we count them blessed who endure. You have heard of the perseverance of Job and seen the end intended by the Lord—that the Lord is very compassionate and merciful. [81]

The book of Job was never intended to be an explanation for suffering. The Apostle James tells us that the intent of the story is to commend Job for His perseverance in his suffering and to show that God is very compassionate and merciful. Whereas most people read the book of Job and focus on the extent of his sufferings, the Holy Spirit, through the Apostle James tells us to look at the *end* of the story. If you think you are a modern day Job, be encouraged! In the end, God turned Job's affliction around and gave him twice as much as he had before! [82]

Many people believe the book of Job teaches that believers should bear their suffering as coming from the hand of the Lord. Although the story does teach us that we should praise God in the midst of our trials, it does not teach us that we should be passive regarding affliction in our lives. In the book of Psalms, God says *"Call on me in the day of trouble and I will deliver you."* [83] God also says *"Many are the afflictions of the righteous, but the Lord delivers him out of them all."* [84] It is interesting to note that Job never calls on God for deliverance. Since the book of Psalms had not yet been written, Job seems to be unaware that God actually delights in delivering his servants from affliction.

Many Christians, like Job, are so convinced that God is the source of their suffering that they never call upon God for deliverance nor do they take their authority to command the devil to take his hands off their lives. They believe that they are called by God to submit to suffering. The problem with this view is that God never requires His children to passively accept suffering in their lives. Although He allows suffering for a reason, He does not expect us to passively accept it as inevitable. In the Bible, it is *always* okay to ask for deliverance. An example of this is the Apostle Paul. Even though Paul was appointed to suffer for the cause of Christ, [85] he still asked his fellow Christians to pray for deliverance from wicked and evil people. [86] When Paul was in prison, he always expected his fellow believers to pray for his release. He also *expected* to be delivered as well. [87] This shows us that, although God wants us to praise Him in the midst of our trials (as Paul and Silas did in the Phillippian jail), He also wants us to expect Him to deliver us from the evil one. Both responses give glory to God and are not antithetical to each other.

I say this because many Christians are confused about how to respond to suffering in their lives. In a sincere effort to bring glory to God, they are afraid to try to change their situation through prayer thinking that this somehow frustrates the process of growth that God intends to bring through their suffering. If you think this way, be assured my friend, you do not have to worry about this. God never gets mad at people who call out to Him for deliverance. In fact He tells us that *"in everything, by prayer and supplication with thanksgiving, let your requests be made known to God."* [88] Even when Paul asked the Lord to remove the *"thorn in his flesh,"* God did not get angry with Paul. He simply told him, *"My grace is sufficient for you."* [89] The proper response to trials and tribulations is to let your request be made known to God, expect in faith for Him to deliver you, and praise Him in the midst of your trouble. Such an approach gives glory to God regardless of the outcome.

Even though Job did not have perfect faith due to his lack of knowledge, it is comforting to know that God vindicated him in the end simply because Job chose to bless God regardless of his circumstances. You and I may or may not have perfect faith either, but if we choose to honor God regardless of the circumstances in our lives, we will fulfill the ultimate purpose in our lives just like Job did—giving glory to God. And though it may seem like no one is watching, we now know the truth. There is more to the circumstances in our lives than what meets the natural eye.

Maybe you are reading this book right now and you find yourself in a time of severe testings and trials in your life. It may seem that there is no meaning or significance to the suffering that you are going through. Perhaps you feel that what you are going through has no lasting significance because it has little impact on the world around you. Be assured, my friend, your life has greater impact than you realize. You do not know who is watching you. Job had no idea that his life was being watched by angels and that his response to his sufferings was being displayed in the heavenly realms. Your suffering is not meaningless. The angels are watching. More importantly, God is watching. And if you will offer sincere worship and praise to Him in the midst of your trial, you will give more glory to Him than you could ever imagine. And when you get to heaven, you will receive a saint's reward.

CHAPTER FIVE

Cloud of Witnesses

*Therefore we also, since we are surrounded by so great a
cloud of witnesses, let us lay aside every weight, and the sin
which so easily ensnares us, and let us run with endurance
the race that is set before us.*
Hebrews 12:1

I would like to begin this chapter by making a simple statement.
Where you are in life today has very little to do with the choices
that you have made. Does this idea sound a little strange? Let's
think about it for a moment. All of us are following in the footsteps,
whether good or bad, of those who have gone before us. Our lives
are the products not only of our own decisions, but the decisions of
those who have lived and died hundreds – even thousands – of years
before you and I drew our first breath. Think for a moment of what
life would be like if Gutenburg had never invented the printing
press or if Thomas Edison had never invented the light bulb. The
fact that you and I can turn on a lamp and enjoy a stimulating book
in the privacy of our homes has nothing to do with the decisions
that we have made. We live in a world shaped by others who have
gone on before us. This is important because too often we as
Americans have a tendency to view our lives as islands to ourselves.
A simple glance at our most treasured values reveals this to be true.

Self-worth. Self-esteem. Self-respect. Be yourself. Believe in your-self. The underlying moral philosophy by which we order our lives is *individualism.* In our thinking, if we succeed in life, it is because we pulled ourselves from our bootstraps and scraped out a mean-ingful existence for ourselves. As Americans, we are told from childhood that our individual lives are what *we* make it to be.

This is in stark contrast to the worldview of millions of people living in Eastern cultures. When my wife and I were missionaries in West Africa, we encountered an entirely different set of philoso-phies and values. Whereas in America the emphasis is on the part over the whole, in Eastern cultures, particularly Africa and Asia, the emphasis is on the whole over the part. Life is viewed in relation to the community. A person bases his or her decisions not on what is good for the individual, but what is good for the community. And not just the community of the present, but the community of the past, present, and future as well. Africans are all too aware that they are living in the land that their ancestors have plowed through blood, sweat, and tears for centuries.

Almost universally in African traditional religions, it is believed that when a person dies, he or she becomes an ancestral spirit who watches and monitors the lives of those still living. When tragedy strikes or a calamity occurs, the first question that goes through a traditional African's mind is often, *"Which ancestor did I offend?"* Often, traditional Africans will go to a witch doctor or a medicine man to determine which ancestor was offended and for what reason. When this is determined, usually a sacrifice or a ritual is prescribed and the ancestor is thought to be appeased.

Although the African traditional view of life after death goes against the biblical view, it does bring up an interesting question: *Are we being watched by those who have gone before us?* The writer of Hebrews seems to think so! Directly after the great "Hall of Faith" passage in Hebrews chapter 11 describing Old Testament heroes, the writer goes on to say,

> *Therefore we also, since we are surrounded by so great a*
> *cloud of witnesses, let us lay aside every weight, and the sin*
> *which so easily ensnares us, and let us run with endurance*

the race that is set before us. [90]

Although this passage can be interpreted figuratively, it is also possible to take this passage at its literal face-value meaning. Consider that in the book of Revelation, the martyred saints cry out to God, *"How long, O Lord, holy and true, until you judge and avenge our blood on those who dwell on the earth?"* [91] According to this passage, the saints that go through the Great Tribulation [92] will have a degree of knowledge about the events that take place on the earth. This tells me that it is possible that departed brothers and sisters in Christ do have a limited knowledge of events that take place on the earth. Since the author of Hebrews is writing to persecuted believers in the first century, it would make sense to say to them, *"Keep running the race! Abraham, Moses, David, and the prophets of the past are cheering you on!"*

Consider also the words of Jesus in Luke 15:10:

"Likewise, I say to you, there is joy in the presence of the angels of God over one sinner who repents."

Think about it. When you lead a person to Christ, angels rejoice! Not only do the angels rejoice, but quite possibly the great heroes of the faith in times past rejoice with you as well. How awesome it is to think that our lives are being watched by saints and angels in heaven!

I suspect that there are many people who are unnoticed on earth but celebrities in heaven. Just as there are "Halls of Fame" for baseball players and rock stars here on earth, I believe that there are "Halls of Faith" in heaven for people who serve Christ faithfully during their earthly lives. Consider what the Word of God says in Daniel 12:3:

Those who are wise shall shine like the brightness of the firmament. And those who turn many to righteousness like the stars forever and ever.

Is it possible that the prophet Daniel is saying there is a degree of status in heaven to those who win souls to the Lord here on earth? If so, then I wonder why so many Christians live their lives for earthly status when they could be pursuing heavenly status?

I find it interesting that, in America, we refer to our celebrities as "stars." It seems that in our celebrity- crazed culture that everyone wants to be a "star" even if it is for only fifteen minutes of fame. To be a "star" is, in a sense, a way of achieving earthly immortality for many people. To many Americans with little or no concept of the primacy of eternity, achieving a degree of fame or recognition in this life (or material goods for that matter) is the only way to trump the seemingly insignificance of their lives. Why else would somebody who knows that they cannot sing subject themselves to the ridicule of the public on American Idol? For many, negative attention is better than no attention at all.

Those who achieve little fame or recognition in their lives often live vicariously through the ones that do. A simple glance of the magazines at the check-out counter of the local grocery store reveals this to be true. Why is it that Americans want to know everything about the lives of their favorite celebrities? To many, the *National Enquirer* is more important than the daily newspaper. Further yet, how about all the award shows that the "stars" throw for themselves? The Grammys. The Oscars. The Emmys. The Peoples' Choice Awards. Country Music Awards… and the list goes on. Why is it that these are the cultural icons of our nation? The British have the Royal family. We have Hollywood. Could it be that the cultural elite of our society represent what we wish for ourselves? Namely, recognition, significance, and earthly immortality?

How sad it is that, in America, our cultural icons are those who heap earthly treasures upon *themselves*! Our icons are Hollywood celebrities, sports stars, and business executives on the cover of Fortune 500 magazines. Even in the Church, I have observed this to be the case. Why is it that when an actor or sports star is converted in this country, they are immediately thrown into the evangelical spotlight? Often, with little time for growth and maturity, the Christian "celebrity" is in more demand than a seasoned Bible teacher. [93] To many, if a Christian quarterback wins the Superbowl, it is viewed on the same level as God sending revival to the country!

Somehow I find it a little difficult to imagine that angels are up in heaven watching the Superbowl cheering on Christian football players! I can imagine, however, all of heaven taking notice when a man or woman forsakes all to take the gospel to a lost tribe that has never heard the name of Jesus. Here is what Gospel for Asia founder K.P. Yohannan has to say on this matter:

> *"Christian magazines, TV shows, and church services often put the spotlight on famous athletes, beauty queens, businessmen, and politicians who 'make it in the world and have Jesus too!'"* [94]

It is a sad commentary to say that, in America, we tend to identify success with status and material goods to the point where acquiring things for self becomes a virtue. Although it is true that God *"gives us all things richly to enjoy,"*[95] we need to keep things in their proper perspective. I was watching a program on television where a news reporter asked a very well-known preacher about his lavish lifestyle. The preacher answered that his executive lifestyle was giving hope to the disenfranchised in his community. The man went on to say that many in his community feel that the only way to gain his degree of wealth is through a life of drugs and violence. Although I do not doubt the sincerity of this preacher, I do think that this man was operating from a false assumption. The assumption is that acquiring things for self is a virtue to be admired and emulated. This is a very prevalent assumption in American Christianity. How many American Christians feel that their witness will not be taken seriously unless they achieve a certain measure of status for themselves? How often do we despise the poor thinking that their faith is of little value because of their position in life? We would do well to heed the admonition of the Apostle James: *"Has God not chosen the poor of this world to be rich in faith and heirs of the kingdom which He promised to those who love Him?"* [96]

I have a feeling that if the Apostle Paul were to walk into most of our churches hungry and destitute from the rigors of his missionary labors, we would probably throw him out of the church and onto the streets! The assumption would be that someone of such low status could not be a true Apostle of God. After all, if he truly had enough faith, wouldn't he be able to at least take care of his own needs? Perhaps this is one of the reasons why third-world missionary agencies are given such little consideration in the missions budgets of most of our churches. When my wife and I were in West Africa, we met a very hard-working group of native evangelists that had been known to sacrifice themselves nearly to the point of starvation in order to advance the gospel to unreached towns and villages. We also heard that these same men had been scolded in the past for a lack of faith by pastors of multi-million dollar church enterprises in America! The assumption was that since they had little, they must have little faith. [97]

How sad it is that Western Christianity equates material success with spiritual success by despising the poor of this world! Are we so satisfied with our fancy buildings, plush carpets, and state-of-the art sound systems that our ears are dull to the cries of untold millions around the world plunging into the gates of hell? I wonder if the Apostle Paul would say the same thing to the average American church as he said to the Corinthian church of his time. *"You are already full! You are already rich! You have reigned as kings without us!"* [98] Worse yet, I wonder if Jesus would say to us what He said to the church of the Laodiceans: *"Because you say, I am rich, have become wealthy, and have need of nothing-and do not know that you are wretched, miserable, poor, blind, and naked."* [99]

I suspect that one of the reasons why most American churches are so self-satisfied is because we, in American, tend to view the gospel as a form of self-improvement. In his book *Revolution in World Missions*, K.P. Yohannan contrasts the typical conversion testimony of those in America with those in the developing two-thirds world.

The typical media testimony goes something like this: "I was sick and broke, a total failure. Then I met Jesus. Now everything is fine. My business is booming and I am a great success. It sounds wonderful. Be a Christian and get that bigger house and a boat and vacation in the Holy Land.

But if that were really God's way, it would put some Christians behind the Iron Curtain and in the Third World in a pretty bad light. Their testimonies often go something like this: "I was happy. I had everything-prestige, recognition, a good job, and a happy wife and children. Then I gave my life to Jesus Christ. Now I am in Siberia, having lost my family, wealth, reputation, job, and health. Here I live lonely, deserted by friends. I cannot see the face of my wife and dear children. My crime is that I love Jesus.[100]

Can you see the difference between the two testimonies? One sees Jesus as a way to self-fulfillment in this life. The other sees Jesus as the door to true riches in the world to come. When the gospel is reduced to merely a vehicle of life enhancement (as it often is in America), acquiring things for self becomes a virtue. People are admired for what they can achieve for themselves. Although this may be a cultural value, it is certainly not a biblical one. The truth is that biblical virtue is marked not by *self-acquisition*, but by *self-sacrifice*.

Look at what the writer of Hebrews has to say about those whom God identifies as the great heroes of faith.

Others were tortured, not accepting deliverance, that they might obtain a better resurrection. Still others had trial of mockings and scourgings, yes, and of chains and imprisonment. They were stoned, they were sawn in two, were tempted, were slain with the sword. They wandered about in sheepskins and goatskins, being destitute, afflicted, tormented-of whom the world was not worthy. They wandered in deserts and mountains, in dens and caves of the earth. [101]

Words such as *destitute, afflicted, and tormented* do not seem to describe the people that the American Church holds up as icons for our culture. We have little respect for *these* types of people who have yet to pull themselves up from their bootstraps to achieve a measure of "success" for themselves. Our heroes are those who make it in *this* world. We are far more interested in going to seminars where we can learn from famous football coaches and business executives on how to be successful in life. Can you imagine a conference in America featuring a speaker who lives in a cave and wanders about preaching the gospel in sheepskins and goatskins? Doubtful. How about a success seminar featuring a peasant evangelist who heals the sick, raises the dead, and oversees thousands of churches? Still doubtful. There are numerous people, men and women, who fit this description in the developing world. Unfortunately, we have very little place in our hearts and minds for understanding them. In building up our own personal kingdoms, we forget that *"the form of this world is passing away."* [102]

Who are the true "stars" in the kingdom of Heaven? The ones whose lives are watched by the great *"cloud of witnesses"* in heaven are those who sacrifice of themselves in order to *"turn many to righteousness."* Those who give of themselves to advance the gospel may never achieve earthly immortality, but rest assured they achieve heavenly immortality.

Think about the widow with two mites as an example. In Luke 21:1-4 we read,

> *And He looked up and saw the rich putting their gifts into the treasury, and He saw also a certain poor widow putting in two mites. So He said, 'Truly I say to you that this poor widow has put in more than all; for all these out of their abundance have put in offerings for God, but she out of her poverty put in all the livelihood that she had.*

Here is a woman that would definitely *not* be a likely candidate for the "Who's Who" list of Christian superstars propped up by Christian magazines and television. Here was a woman out of a husband, out of a job, and out of luck. Not only was she a widow, but a very *poor* widow. Regardless of what some say, this poor widow did not give her last two pennies in the offering box in expectation of a "hundred fold" return.[102] Her generosity was based on pure devotion to God. Nothing else. What this woman did receive in return was the respect and admiration of the king of the universe! We do not know for certain whether the great *"cloud of witnesses"* in heaven was watching this woman on that day, but one thing is for certain-Jesus was watching! I have a feeling that there will be many "poor widows" in heaven who lived their lives in relative obscurity on earth while giving sacrificially for the sake of the gospel. I have a feeling that these are the ones who will be in the heavenly hall of fame.

I imagine that the rich putting their gifts into the treasury were feeling pretty good about themselves until Jesus shattered their self-righteousness by acknowledging the gift of a poor, despised widow. Do we have a parallel in the Church today? Consider the region of the world known as the 10/40 Window for example. The 10/40 Window is a geographic region of the world that describes the area from West Africa and East Asia from 10 degrees north of the equator to 40 degrees north of the equator. It includes all of West Africa, North Africa, the Middle East, Central Asia, and the Far East region of Asia. Ninety five percent of the people living in this region of the world are unevangelized. Many have never heard the gospel even once. It is also the center of the world's population. Two thirds of the world's population, more than 3.2 billion people, live in the 10/40 Window. It is the home of the world's greatest poverty. Eighty-five percent of those living in the 10/40 Window are considered the poorest of the poor in the world. This region of the world is also the birthplace and the center of the world's greatest non-Christian religions, namely Buddhism, Hinduism, and Islam. Given the gravity of the situation, you would think that evangelizing the people living in this region of the world would be top priority to churches in the West. Certainly this is the case, right? Wrong. According to Bryant Myers of World Vision, only about 1.25% of Christian mission giving is going to missionary work in the 10/40 Window. [103]

Much of the work in this region of the world is actually being done by native evangelists. Native evangelists are Christian laborers indigenous to the countries or regions where they are working. They are often very poor and despised by their own friends and family because of their stand for the gospel. Many of them sacrifice prestige and privilege for the sake of the gospel. Most sacrifice their own physical health because of the rigors of their missionary labors. Almost without exception, all pay a price to plant churches in towns and villages where none yet exist. While we are busy congratulating ourselves for our multi-million dollar church buildings, these penniless preachers are quietly turning the world upside down through their self-sacrifice. While we are busy gorging ourselves with Christian conferences, seminars, books, music, magazines, radio, and television, we are giving our pocket change to the 3.2 billion people of the world who live in regions where the gospel has yet to penetrate. While everyone in America has thousands of opportunities to hear the gospel through various avenues, many in the world have yet to hear it for the first time.

Such a gross unbalance undoubtedly grieves the heart of God. If Jesus suffered so great a sacrifice for us, should we not also be willing to sacrifice for the people He loves? If Jesus truly is the *"propitiation not only for our sins, but also for the sins of the whole world,"* [104] then why isn't evangelizing the *"whole world"* a priority for most American Christians? I understand the "out of sight, out of mind" principle. People are normally not moved by things distant from the world in which they live. However, sometimes I think that we do not see because we do not want to see. Closing our eyes to the spiritual needs of two-thirds of the world's population is not going to make the problem go away. I wonder how this tragic imbalance looks from the perspective of the great *"cloud of witnesses"* in heaven? We cry out to God for revival, but are we revived to the needs of those who may never have a chance to hear the gospel unless we in the West begin to put feet to our prayers?

I believe that the Spirit is saying to the Church in America today, *"Awake, you who sleep"* to the needs of the lost. *"Arise from the dead, and Christ will give you light."* [105] I believe that it is up to us to wake *ourselves* to the needs of the lost. When we awake to the needs of the world and arise to take the gospel to those who have not yet heard, then Christ will give us light on how we are to fulfill the Great Commission in our generation.

CHAPTER SIX

While There Is Still Time

But this I say, brethren, the time is short...
I Corinthians 7:29

The year 2000 has come and gone, and here we stand on the brink of a new millennium. Although we have experienced an unprecedented growth in knowledge of the world through science and technology, many of the basic questions of life remain unanswered in the hearts and minds of this generation. *What is the meaning of life? Who am I? Why am I here and where am I going?* Although these questions have troubled the hearts of men and women ever since the beginning of time, it seems that this generation is asking questions even beyond the philosophical norms. In a world of disease, crime, famine, war, terrorism, and weapons of mass destruction, we in this generation are daily faced with the one inescapable question: *Is there really any hope for humanity?*

Since the question of our destiny is a difficult one. It is crucial that we, the people of this generation, begin to face the issue of our role in the scheme of history. Are we simply repeating the cycles of generations long past, or do we as a generation have a specific destiny and a specific purpose for a specific time? To put it simply, are we merely an extension of the past or a springboard to the future? These are very hard questions to ask; yet the difficult questions are often the most critical.

Before coming to grips with our place in the scheme of history, we must first be willing to take a cold, hard look at our generation and the world in which we live. The heart-wrenching truth of the matter is this: Problems in this world have not gotten any better but are constantly getting worse. Drugs, prostitution, and violence ravage our streets and destroy countless numbers of lives every day. Parents live in fear for the safety of their sons and daughters, wondering if their children could be the next victims of another high school massacre. To make matters worse, the post-Cold War world in which we live seems to be crumbling all around us. Our dreams of a comfortable world were shattered as we watched in horror as two jet airplanes flew into the Word Trade Center.

Although we thought that technology could solve our problems, we came to realize that technology has simply made us more sophisticated at committing evil. Now, instead of swords, arrows, and spears, we use tanks, bombs, and weapons of mass destruction. We thought that human government would solve our problems only to find out that the law is powerless to change the nature of a man. Though we try to console ourselves with the idea that society is progressing, we are forced to face the facts that our prisons are still full, terrorists are lurking around the corner in our own backyards, and our streets and schools are not getting any safer.

Strangely, the very thing that we think can save us is often the very problem that destroys us. We seek to find an escape through acquiring material possessions and, as a result, we work our lives to gain what we can never keep. It seems that the American dream is flashed before us in every billboard, in every popular song on the radio, in every TV commercial and in every Internet advertisement saying, *"You can have it all—right here, right now. Grab all you can. You only live once!"* But when the clothes fade and the cars wax old, we are once again faced with the reality that we can take nothing with us when we die. [106]

Those of us who embrace Jesus Christ as Lord and Savior have watched our generation waste its life away through drugs, sex, and alcohol. The mindset of our peers is, *"Eat, drink, and be merry, for tomorrow we die!"* And yet they never seem to realize that those who live by the bottle will die by the bottle.

The moral depravity of our generation is so immense that we, as Christians, have often looked the other way in an attempt to forget about the reality that we see. Another life destroyed by drugs, another teenage pregnancy, another unsuspecting girl caught in an abusive relationship, another suicide, another family ripped apart by adultery, another divorce… and the list goes on.

It seems that we are always searching for something greater than ourselves—something to give our lives a sense of purpose and destiny. We have stood in the shadows of our fathers and grandfathers who fought so bravely to preserve the freedom that we now enjoy. While the World War II generation has been labeled the Great Generation because of its self-sacrifice and heroism, we have been labeled the Columbine Generation because of our violence and materialism. We seem to measure up to the very lack of expectations imposed on us. Where are the dreamers in our generation? Where have all the prophets gone? Generations in the past believed that they could change the world. We on the other hand have a hard time believing that our own lives and communities can change, much less the world. Drugs, crime, rebellion, and materialism. What can it all mean but that we as a generation are void of a cause worth dying for?

The problem with our generation goes deeper than drugs, alcohol, violence, and moral laxity. Although these problems are very real, they are merely symptoms of a much deeper issue. The real problem of our generation is that we are a generation without a vision. We have nothing to stand for that we deem worthy enough to unite ourselves under a common objective. The generation of the Sixties were rebels with a cause, but we are warriors without. And because of our lack of vision, we are perishing in our own vanity.

This brings us to the heart of the matter. What dream can possibly be worthy enough to unite an entire generation of millions of individuals across the globe to save us from this dungeon of restlessness? The answer lies not in our fanciful imaginations, but in the very heart of God Himself.

Ever since the scattering of the nations at the tower of Babel, [107] God has been consumed with passion for one cause and one cause alone—to bring glory to Himself by uniting a people out of every tongue, tribe, and nation. After the scattering of the peoples at the tower of Babel, the heart of God for the nations was so consumed with love that He gave an immutable, unchangeable oath to one man—Abraham. In Genesis 12:1-3, God promised Abraham that He would *bless him and make him a great nation. He would bless those that blessed him and curse those that cursed him and, in his seed, all the nations of the earth would be blessed.* Throughout the rest of human history, even up to the very hour in which we live, God has been actively working on fulfilling His promise to Abraham that, in his seed, all the nations of the earth would be blessed.

The cross-cultural aspect of the Great Commission began not at the end of the four gospels, but four thousand years ago for Abraham and his seed to bless every language and people group with the knowledge of salvation. We, as the spiritual seed of Abraham, have been given the awesome responsibility of seeing to it that every distinct ethnic people is blessed with the knowledge of salvation through Jesus Christ. [108]

Not only is the Great Commission the central core to the heart of God in human history, it is also a direct, nonnegotiable command from Jesus Christ Himself. Jesus said, *"Go therefore and make disciples of all nations."* [109] Our Lord and Savior did not give us a command that is impossible to fulfill. I believe that if a task is definable, then it is achievable. According to many leading missiologists, there remain approximately 10,000 people groups with no viable witness of Jesus Christ and no access to the gospel.[110] If we, as a generation, will prayerfully send out missionaries to plant reproducing churches among the remaining 10,000 unreached people groups of the earth, we will have completed the Great Commission! What can possibly be a greater cause than the very purpose for which God Himself has been working for the past 4,000 years to fulfill? Think about the opportunity presented to us. For the first time in four thousand years, there is a generation that can actually bring closure and completion to the Great Commission! And we are privileged to be that generation!

If it was the Great Commission that drove Christ to the cross, then it will be the Great Commission that drives our generation to the altar of sacrifice and courage. Jesus said, *"If I be lifted up, I will draw all men to myself."*[111] Although we tend to think of this verse in the context of our worship services, what Jesus was actually saying was that if He would be lifted up on the cross, He would draw all distinct, ethnic peoples to Himself. If the Great Commission is a cause worthy enough for Jesus Christ to shed His blood on the cross, then it is a cause worthy enough to give our lives to complete.

Men and women of this generation, look at Christ who was cursed by God on the cross and made a reproach among men for our sakes! Perhaps you will see the tears flowing from His eyes, as there are still two billion people cut off from the gospel! [112]

Although it has been said that the Bible predicts a great world-wide harvest of souls before the return of Christ, I have come to wonder if perhaps the state of the world before the great and terrible Day of the Lord [113] is largely up to us. If we, like the Apostle John, could lay our heads on the chest of Christ, perhaps we could still hear his heart beating today. *That none should perish. That none should perish.* [114]

The task has been defined. The clock is ticking. In view of God's impending wrath and His enduring love for all mankind, let us complete the Great Commission before it is too late. The world is waiting for us. The great cloud of witnesses in heaven is crying out to us today. Can you hear Abraham, Moses, David, and Paul crying out to us from heaven? Saints and angels are crying out to us today: "Finish the task! Finish the task! While there is still time!"

CHAPTER 7

Reflections

*How then shall they call on Him in whom they have not
believed? And how shall they believe in whom they have not
heard? And how shall they hear without a preacher? And
how shall they preach unless they are sent?*
Romans 10:14-15

In contemplating the subject matter of this book, I have found
myself hard-pressed between the desires both to comfort the
afflicted and to afflict the comfortable. Although it may seem at
times that I am overly critical of the American Church for its pride
and materialism, in actuality, I love the American church and the
American culture. Having said this, I must also say that, as a young
evangelist, I have observed some trends in the American Church
that deeply concern me. Much has been said recently about the
explosion of evangelical Christianity in the popular media culture.
It seems that God is now a big business in America. Although many
see this as a sign of revival, I am not so sure. It seems that the
majority of what is being passed off as "gospel" in popular
Christian media is little more than Christian life enhancement.
While this may be legitimate for Christians, is it enough to save the
lost in our culture?

The new rule in American preaching according to the latest

church growth theories is that all preaching must be positive, relevant, and pertaining to the felt needs of those who hear the
message. It is often said that ministers should not be answering
questions that people are not asking. My question is, "Do people
really know what they *should* be asking?" Most people are more
concerned with the question of *"How do I make my life better"*
than *"How can I, a sinner, be justified before a holy and righteous
God?"* It stands to reason that a gospel of life improvement will
always be more popular than a gospel of sin, judgement, grace, and
repentance. I fear that in our attempt to be culturally relevant, we
are becoming biblically irrelevant.

Consider what the Apostle Paul says in I Thessalonians 1:9-10:

> *For they themselves declare concerning us what manner of
> entry we had to you, and how you turned to God from idols
> to serve the living and true God, and to wait for His Son
> from heaven, whom He raised from the dead, even Jesus,
> who delivers us from the wrath to come.*

Here Paul is reminding the Thessalonian Christians of the basic
gospel that he preached to them in the beginning. Notice that Paul
did not present the gospel to the Thessalonians as a way of fixing
their broken lives. Paul's original message to the Thessalonians was,
*"Repent and turn to Jesus! Only He can deliver you from the wrath
to come!"* My gut instinct tells me that a title like this would probably never make the New York Times Bestseller list. Sin, death, hell,
and judgement will never be a *positive* message, but it will always be
essential to the preaching of the gospel if we are to follow the example of the Apostles. The very first evangelistic message ever
preached was not, "There is an emptiness in your heart that only
Jesus can fill," but *"Be saved from this perverse generation."*[115]

Perhaps the fact that Jesus talked more about hell than He did
about heaven had something to do with the sense of urgency
displayed in the preaching of the early Apostles. How often is this
sense of urgency displayed in Christian preaching today?
Regretfully, the answer is very little. It seems that we are more
interested in blessing the saved than saving the lost.

Worse yet, how often do we in America see the simple preaching of the gospel demonstrated with signs, wonders, and miracles? While it is certain that there have been extremes in this area in the past, it seems that few in America expect miracles of healing and deliverance to accompany the preaching of the gospel anymore. We expect these things to happen overseas, but not here in the enlightened West. Whereas in the New Testament, it would have been considered normal for the preaching of the gospel to be accompanied by miracles, in America today we consider such a demonstration abnormal. I have noticed that, in America, it is even fashionable to downplay the supernatural—especially when it comes to healings and miracles. I wonder what the Apostle Paul would say to us today about our lack of faith in the miraculous? Probably the same thing he said to the Corinthians of his own day.

And I, brethren, when I came to you, did not come with excellence of speech or of wisdom declaring to you the testimony of God. For I determined not to know anything among you except Jesus Christ and Him crucified. I was with you in weakness, in fear, and in much trembling. And my speech and my preaching were not with persuasive words of human wisdom, but in demonstration of the Spirit and of power, that your faith should not be in the wisdom of men but in the power of God. [116]

It seems that we have a lot of *"excellence of speech"* but very little *"demonstration of the Spirit and power"* in the American Church today. I wonder if this is the Christianity that Jesus had in mind when He said the words, *"Most assuredly, I say to you, he who believes in Me, the works that I do he will do also; and greater works than these he will do, because I go to my Father."* [117] The Apostles would have understood this to mean that, through faith in Jesus, they would be able to heal the sick and cast out devils just as they saw Jesus doing throughout His earthly ministry. How easily we invent theories to explain away verses like these in order to soothe our unbelief! This problem is not limited to those who take a view of the Scriptures that the gifts of the Holy Spirit have passed away. If we look at much of what comes on Christian television today, it seems that, nowadays, even Pentecostals and Charismatics are more interested in claiming blessings for themselves than applying the power of God to heal the sick and save the lost. [118]

Perhaps a lack of power in ministry is one of the reasons why American Evangelicals are so easily sidetracked when it comes to focusing on the essentials of the Great Commission. According to Jesus, the essence of the Great Commission is, *"Go. Preach the gospel. And make disciples of all nations."* [119] It is precisely the Great Commission that teaches us that people of all races and colors are equally valuable in the sight of God. While this truth may seem self-evident to most American Christians, a failure to understand this can lead to atrocities of the worst kind. I have in mind the horrific genocide that took place in the country of Rwanda in 1994. Within a short period of time, roughly one million ethnic Tutsis were slaughtered by the Hutu people. The tragedy of this situation is that this was a country with an overwhelming "Christian" majority. How could this be? Christians killing Christians! Many were even using the Bible to justify their actions! If Christians worldwide would take seriously the cross-cultural dimension of the Great Commission, tragedies like these would be avoided. A glorious vision of people of all races, tribes, and colors worshiping at the feet of Jesus precludes racism and prejudice.

Although the tragedy in Rwanda is an extreme example, it would be a wise course of action to examine our own hearts for hatred and prejudice. Of particular concern is the way many American Christians view the Arab people. Since September 11, our Christian bookstores have been flooded with one-sided authors portraying the Israeli/Palestinian conflict in overly simplistic terms. Too often, Arabs are portrayed as "sons of Ishmael" and "enemies of the people of God" in popular Christian literature. My heart cringes when I hear overzealous preachers describing the current conflict as the inevitable byproduct of Abraham's tragic mistake of producing Ishmael. The thinking goes that just as Ishmael was a troublemaker to Isaac, so the Arab people are destined to be troublemakers to the people of God for all time. [120] Such an oversimplification of terms should give us all a warning call for pause and reflection. It was precisely because of similar interpretations of passages in the Old Testament that gave white Americans a justification for enslaving black Americans in times past. Thankfully, the Church has made much progress in dealing with racism concerning African Americans. We no longer believe that black people are under the curse of Ham.[121] If we are not careful, we may repeat the same mistake of the past by misapplying the Scriptures to justify racism against Arabs living in our country and abroad.

While it is true that God has a special plan for the Jewish people in the end-times, it is equally true that Christ has *"broken down the middle wall of separation"* [122] between Jew and Gentile. This leaves no room for ethnic superiority in the Body of Christ. All are equally lost and equally forgiven in Christ. The way that some ultra-fundamentalist preachers talk, it would seem that Jesus died for everybody but the Palestinians! Very few American Christians even realize that there is a significant population of Christians among the Palestinian people and the Arab world at large. In fact, many Arabs in America are Christians who have come here in order to flee persecution in the Middle East. Many of them have been made to feel like second-class citizens in the Kingdom of God by American Christians.

Not only are Arab Christians in America made to feel inferior because of ignorance and prejudice, the situation is far worse among Palestinian Christians. It is estimated that just over two percent of Palestinians living in the Middle East today are actually Christians, not Muslims. [123] Have we forgotten that Jesus said the way the world would know His true disciples is by their love for each other? [124] Are Palestinian Christians not our brothers and sisters also? Our love for the brethren should include Arabs, and, yes, Palestinians as well as Jews.

I think that Christians should rightly question interpretations of Scripture that oversimplify matters by failing to recognize that both sides have suffered injustices in this conflict. Simple common sense should tell us that injustice is rarely ever one-sided. Jesus said, *"Blessed are the peacemakers for they shall be called sons of God."* [124] How can we be peacemakers when we blindly support only one side of the conflict? How can the world possibly take us seriously when we have Christian fundamentalist groups prolonging the conflict by raising millions of dollars to fund Jewish settlers in the West Bank? Should this really be a priority when approximately two-thirds of the world's population lives in regions of the world where the gospel has yet to penetrate? Let's think about this for a moment. While dedicated native evangelists in India and Africa are sacrificing themselves to the point of starvation to plant churches in unreached towns and villages with little to no support from the West, big named ministries in America somehow feel it is a greater priority to fuel hatred in the Muslim world by driving people out of a land they have inhabited for centuries.

While it is true that, in the Old Testament, God promised the land of Canaan to the Jewish people as an everlasting possession, nowhere in the New Testament does Jesus give His followers a mandate to reclaim the Promised Land for Israel. In fact, when His disciples did ask Him when He was going to restore the kingdom to Israel, His answer was, *"It is not for you to know times or seasons which the Father has put under His own authority. But you shall receive power when the Holy Spirit has come upon you; and you shall be witnesses to me in Jerusalem, and in all Judea, and Samaria, and to the end of the earth."* [125] Jesus was essentially saying to His disciples, *"Don't worry about when the Old Testament prophecies concerning Israel will come to pass. You focus on your job description and let God take care of the rest."* As the Church of Jesus Christ, our job description is to *"Go and make disciples of all nations."* [126] How easily we are distracted from the work of the Great Commission! I have even heard of Christians breeding red heifers for the purpose of restoring Solomon's temple! I suspect that if God wants to expand the borders of Israel, He is well capable of doing so when Jesus returns. But as long as we are on this side of eternity, Christians should seek for solutions that respect the rights and dignity of people on all sides of the conflict.

It is the tendency to neglect the Great Commission by getting sidetracked on peripheral issues that I find the most troubling in the American Church. Too often, we are more concerned with chasing doctrinal fads than evangelizing the lost. Having said this, I do believe that most American Christians are generous people who love God and genuinely desire to help others. The same is true for most pastors as well. The problem is that most Americans have very little knowledge about the rest of the world and are therefore unaware of their privileged status in the world.

When my wife and I were missionaries among the Muslim and animist peoples of West Africa, we were amazed at the lengths that people would go to obtain a visa for America. We saw many young people putting their entire lives on hold for the pipe dream of coming to America. Often perfect strangers would come up to us asking if we could write a letter to our embassy for them to obtain a visa to the U.S. For many, it seemed like crossing the Atlantic was equivalent to crossing the Jordan.

Although my wife and I are fairly young in age, between the two of us, we have traveled much of Africa, Asia, and Latin America. We have seen some of the poorest of the poor in the world. We have seen people living in cardboard boxes scraping by on a bowl of rice a day. We have seen naked children gladly accepting leftover chicken bones as if it were ice cream or cotton candy. We have come to realize that most of our modern American conveniences (such as heating and air conditioning, owning our own homes and vehicles, and quick access to capital) are far removed from the daily realities of the vast majority of people living in the world. My guess is that our lower middle class lives better than 90 percent of people in the world today.

Not only are we the wealthiest of the wealthy, we also live in relative peace and security. Although September 11th shook us up as a nation, the majority of us were unaffected. Most of us went on with our comfortable lives as if nothing had ever happened. We easily forget that war and unrest are living, daily realities to many in the developing world. I have seen the death camps of Auschwitz. I have seen the prison torture museums of Cambodia. I have known young male children selling themselves into prostitution so that they could provide for their families. Moreover, I have visited Christians living in countries where one could suffer years of imprisonment and torture simply for sharing their faith. In contemplating the poverty and misery of so many people living in third world countries, I cannot help but ask myself, *"Why did God allow me to be born and raised in America, the most privileged nation in the world?"*

This question should stir us all to pause and reflection. Whether we realize it or not, we have more privileges and opportunities than the vast majority of people living in the world. Sometimes I wonder what my life would be like if I was raised in a war-torn country in abject poverty. The obvious answer is that life would be miserable. Being raised in a Christian family, I have no idea what it would be like to be beaten and thrown in jail by my own parents simply for professing faith in Christ. I daresay that few in America have suffered total and complete ostracism from their families simply for deciding to become a Christian. In most countries in the 10/40 Window, even the ones that do not have official government persecution, such an experience would be considered a normal part of Christian conversion.

Sometimes I wonder why Christians in the West live in such comfort and security while Christians in the rest of the world are struggling to survive in the face of discrimination and persecution. I am reminded of the incident in the gospel of John where Peter, after being told by Jesus that he was destined to face a painful and miserable death for the sake of the gospel, asked Jesus what was to become of the Apostle John. Jesus responded by telling Peter, *"If I will that he remains till I come, what is that to you?"* [127] Jesus seemed to make no apology for the fact that some believers will have to pay a higher price for their faith than others.

I say this because often Christians in the West feel guilty for their comfortable lives while the rest of the Body of Christ is suffering from persecution and poverty. While the guilt approach may motivate a few Christians to help our suffering brethren worldwide, I do not believe this is the best approach. God does not ask us to feel guilty for being blessed. This would make God appear to be double-minded if He blessed people and nations only to make them guilty for receiving the blessings. It also robs God of His pleasure in showering gifts upon His children. Instead, the Bible says that God *"gives us richly all things to enjoy."* [128] God takes pleasure when His children enjoy the blessings He gives them.

A better approach is a sense of responsibility that springs from a heart of gratefulness. Because God has blessed us, we have a responsibility to pass our blessings along to others. If God has prospered us in the West, then His prosperity is for a purpose. God blessed Abraham so that he could be a blessing to the nations. [129] The same is true today. God saves us, heals us, and prospers us so that we can be a blessing to the nations. It is when we sacrifice ourselves to help those different than us that God is truly glorified in the presence of the angels. This is the beauty of the Great Commission. In a world of racism and prejudice, the Great Commission provides Christians with the motivation to lay down their pride and serve those whom their culture teaches to fear and despise. I can only imagine what it looks like from the perspective of heaven when whites embrace blacks, Bosnians embrace Serbians, and Jews embrace Palestinians. Only the love of Jesus makes this possible. A passion for the glory of God in the hearts of Christians is the only real hope for peace in the world today.

A vision such as this must be translated into concrete action if it is to progress beyond an idealistic dream. As the Apostle John reminds us,

> *But whoever has this world's goods and sees his brother in need, and shuts up his heart from him, how does the love of God abide in Him? My little children, let us not love in word or in tongue, but in deed and in truth.* [130]

We in the West are those who have this world's goods. Believers living in the 10/40 Window are those in need. If we in America really believe that an African soul or an Asian soul is equally valuable in the eyes of God as an American soul, then it is our obligation to help our brothers and sisters living in the world's neediest region to reach their nations for Christ.

It also means that we have to understand that the role of the Western Church has changed from that of a pioneer to the role of a servant. There was a time in the past when most of the pioneer missions in the world were by Western missionaries and agencies. That time has now passed. Since the collapse of colonialism and the rise of the nation-state, native evangelists are doing most of the pioneer evangelism in the world today. Native evangelists are gospel workers either native to or similar to the people or country in which they are working. Since native evangelists live at or near the level of the people they serve, they are far more cost effective and culturally relevant for church planting work. Whereas it costs an average of $3,000-$5,000 a month to support a Western missionary, the cost is usually $100-$500 a month to support a native evangelist.

In general, when it comes to pioneer church planting, they can do far more in far less time than an average Western missionary can. Since they already know the language and the culture, they can present the gospel in a culturally relevant way without being perceived as messengers of a foreign imperialistic religion. Since many countries in the 10/40 Window are officially closed to foreign missionaries, native evangelists can often go where Western missionaries cannot go.

When my wife and I were missionaries in West Africa, we saw first hand the efficiency of native evangelists. While we were living comfortably on support from our friends and family back home, we saw native evangelists doing far more than what we could do with little to no support. We also saw how much more they could accomplish if they only had someone to come alongside and help them do what they could not. One pastor living in the southern part of Senegal wanted to take our twenty-year-old Toyota Land Cruiser to go out into the remote villages to visit the cell groups he had started. We begged him not to take it because of all the mechanical problems it had given us. The pastor proceeded to tell us that he needed the vehicle. After reluctantly giving him the vehicle, he joyfully took it back to his region. We still receive phone calls and e-mails from him thanking us for giving him the vehicle.

Our missionary friends in the country of Guinea Bissau have similar stories to tell. In Guinea Bissau, a country where half the population is Muslim and the other half is animist (African traditional religion), Muslim village chiefs have approached them begging for missionaries to come to their villages. Their response was that they would like to send workers, but there were not enough trained workers to send. Imagine that. Muslim village leaders begging for missionaries! Jesus knew exactly what He was saying when He said, *"The harvest is plentiful, but the laborers are few."* [131]

On one visit to Guinea Bissau, my wife and I saw a Muslim village with an abandoned church building. Our missionary friends explained to us that, at one time, the church was thriving under the work of a Brazilian missionary. When the missionary left and went back to Brazil, there was no one to carry on the work, so the church eventually died. When I asked my friends if there was anyone left from the church that was still faithful to the Lord, they told me that there was a young man who had remained faithful and desired to revive the church. At that time, a well respected native worker was getting ready to open up a Bible school in the town of Gabu (the largest town in that region). Our ministry immediately provided the funds for this young man to go to the school on a work scholarship basis in partnership with my missionary friends. The last report I received from my missionary friends is that this young man has gone back to his village and has successfully revived the church.

Our ministry also sponsors a young man who has recently started a church in a Muslim village in the eastern region of the country. Within six months, he already has 21 converts. Another worker we support was recently offered a facility to start a Bible School. Because of the support, he was able to move into the facility without having to worry about the transportation costs of sending his daughter to school. Without the support, he said that he would not have been able to move into the facilities. Now he is preparing a program to train workers to plant churches throughout the western region of the country. It is amazing how a little assistance like this can go such a long way to further the kingdom of God in third world countries.

There are countless more opportunities to assist our brothers and sisters in Christ in furthering the gospel throughout the 10/40 Window. I believe that the most effective ministries in the 21st century will be the ones that seek to provide tools and assistance to native evangelists working in the least evangelized areas of the world. Simple things such as purchasing bicycles, gospel cassettes, evangelistic literature, film projectors, and P.A. systems can have far reaching effects if put in the hands of those committed to carrying the gospel to their own people. In countries with official government persecution, Bibles and training materials are the desperate need of the hour. If the Great Commission is to be completed in our generation, then we in the West are going to have to seriously evaluate how we are using our resources for the advancement of the kingdom of God. Investing millions of dollars in state-of-the-art sound equipment may drive our egos, but it will do nothing to evangelize the two billion people who have yet to hear the gospel.

We need to let the words of the Apostle Paul sink into our souls.

How then shall they call on Him in whom they have not believed? And how shall they believe in whom they have not heard? And how shall they hear without a preacher? And how shall they preach unless they are sent? [132]

Jesus said, *"Go into all the world and preach the gospel."* [133] Those who do not go are obligated to send a substitute. Those who desire to hasten the return of Christ should remember that Jesus said, *"And this gospel of the kingdom will be preached in all the world as a witness to all the nations, and then the end will come."* [134] Breeding red heifers will not hasten the return of Christ. Preaching the gospel and sending laborers will. Heaven is waiting. The angels are watching. Who will respond? Only time will tell. See you at the finish line!

How to Be Saved

If you have been touched by this book but have not yet received Jesus Christ as Lord and Savior, I urge you to do so. Although you may think that you are a good person, the Bible says, "There is none righteous. No not one" (Romans 3:10). On a human level, this may seem like a harsh statement. But the fact of the matter is that our understanding of goodness and God's understanding of goodness are two totally different things. A simple glance at the Ten Commandments reveals this to be true. Have you ever told a lie? If you have, then according to God, that makes you a liar. Have you ever committed adultery? You may answer no to that question, but, according to Jesus, if a man even looks at a woman for the purpose of lusting after her, then he commits adultery in his own heart (Matthew 5:28). Also, any willful voluntary sexual intercourse outside of marriage is considered fornication in the eyes of God. The Bible says there will be no fornicators in heaven (Revelation 22:15, I Corinthians 6:9, Ephesians 5:5). Perhaps you have never fornicated, but have you ever had hatred in your heart for somebody? If you have, then according to Jesus, you have committed murder in your own heart (Matthew 5:21-22). Have you ever coveted somebody else's possessions? If you have, the Bible says that no covetous person will inherit the kingdom of God (I Corinthians 6:10, Ephesians 5:5). Have you ever taken the Lord's name in vain? If you have, then you have broken the third commandment, and God calls that blasphemy (Exodus 20:7, II Timothy 3:2). If you have broken any one of these laws mentioned above, then according to the Bible, you are a lawbreaker and a criminal in the eyes of God. The Bible says, "For whoever shall keep the whole law, and yet stumble in one point, he is guilty of all"(James 2:10).

Here is the bottom line: If you want to get to heaven by being a good person, you have to be perfect. Jesus said, "Therefore, you shall be perfect, just as your Father in heaven is perfect" (Matthew 5:48).

The bad news is that because of God's standards of goodness and holiness, just one sin will keep a person out of heaven forever. The Bible teaches that the wages of sin is death (Romans 6:23). What this means is that because you are a sinner, Satan, the one who has power over death (Hebrews 2:14), has a legal right to keep you separated from your loving Heavenly Father and to take you to hell with him when you die (Revelation 20:11-15).

Here is the good news. The Bible says, "God so loved the world that He sent His only begotten Son that whoever believes in Him should not perish but have everlasting life" (John 3:16). Salvation is a free gift! You cannot earn it or deserve it. The Bible says, "For by grace you have been saved through faith, and that not of yourselves; it is the gift of God, not of works, lest anyone should boast" (Ephesians 2:8).

The Bible teaches that "God is love" (I John 4:9). Love is not something that God possesses; it is who God is. Because of His love for you, God sent His Son Jesus into the world to die on the cross in your place and to bear the penalty for your sin. When Jesus was on the cross, the Bible says, "God was in Christ reconciling the world to Himself" (2 Corinthians 5:19). Jesus bore the judgement for your sin and for my sin so that we do not have to suffer the penalty of death, hell, and damnation. The prophet Isaiah says it this way, "All we like sheep have gone astray; we have turned, every one, to his own way; and the Lord has laid on Him the iniquity of us all" (Isaiah 53:6).

Not only did Jesus die on the cross to bear the penalty for your sins, He also rose from the dead so that you can have a new life in

Him (Romans 6:4, Ephesians 2:1-7). The Bible says, "Therefore, If anyone is in Christ, he is a new creation; old things have passed away; behold, all things have become new" (2 Corinthians 5:17). When you are born again, God creates a new man on the inside of you in true righteousness and holiness (Ephesians 4:24). As believers in Christ, we also know that because Christ is risen from the dead, one day He will come back for us and give us a body like His own resurrected glorious body (Philippians 3:20-21). This is what the Apostle Peter refers to as the "living hope" of the resurrection (I Peter 1:3). Jesus said, "Because I live, you will live also" (John 14:19). I have good news for you today. Jesus lives! Though it may seem at times that all hell has broken loose on your life, Jesus lives! And because He lives, you can live also. This hope is not a fool's hope. Over 500 people saw Jesus alive and well after His death on the cross (I Corinthians 15:1-8). Many of them, in fact, are named specifically in the New Testament. This is far beyond what is needed to establish credible testimony in any court of law. God wants us to be sure that the resurrection of Jesus from the dead is no myth or fairy tale (Luke 1:1-4).

Friend, you have a choice today. You can choose to serve self and perish, or you can choose to serve Christ and live. God says, "I call heaven and earth as witnesses today against you, that I have set before you life and death, blessing and cursing; therefore choose life, that both you and your descendants may live" (Deuteronomy 30:19). If you would like to choose life today, God tells you very specifically what you need to do in His Word. The Bible says, "That if you confess with your mouth the Lord Jesus and believe in your heart that God has raised Him from the dead, you will be saved. For with the heart one believes unto righteousness, and with the mouth confession is made unto salvation" (Romans 10:9-10). If you follow God's instructions, rest assured, you will be saved. Remember that when you confess Jesus as Lord, you are telling Him that you are willing to turn from sin and to follow Him. This is what the Bible calls repentance. This does not mean that you have to be perfect to be a Christian. It simply means that you are willing to let Jesus have control of your life. Jesus said, "Why do you call me 'Lord, Lord,' and not do the things which I say?"(Luke 6:46). When you receive

Jesus into your heart, you may still struggle with sin, but God will be in you to help you live the life that He wants you to live.

Friend, only Jesus can save you from the wrath of God (Romans 5:9). The Bible says, "There is no other name under heaven given among men by which we must be saved" (Acts 4:12). The Scriptures also tell us that "whoever calls on the name of the Lord shall be saved" (Romans 10:13). Based on the authority of the Word of God, I can tell you with absolute certainty that if you call on the name of the Lord Jesus Christ today in sincere repentance and faith, you will be saved.

If you are ready to make the choice to receive Jesus into your heart as Lord and Savior, I suggest that you pray a simple prayer such as this:

Jesus, come into my heart. Forgive me of my sins. I accept you.

If you prayed this prayer in sincere faith and repentance, welcome to the family of God! Jesus said, "Behold I stand at the door and knock. If anyone hears My voice and opens the door, I will come in to him and dine with him, and he with me" (Revelation 3:20). If you have sincerely asked Jesus to come and live in your heart, you are now a child of God with full rights and privileges as a citizen of the kingdom of heaven (John 1:12, Philippians 3:20). I suggest you begin reading the New Testament to begin finding out all that is available to you in your new life with Christ. I'll give you a little hint—it is far more than you currently realize!

Along with reading the Bible and talking to God daily, be assured that God also wants you to join a local fellowship of believers. This is absolutely essential if you want to grow in your faith and if you have truly made Jesus Christ the Lord of your life. The Bible tells us not to forsake assembling ourselves together with other believers (Hebrews 10:25). The Apostle John also says, "We know that we have passed from death to life, because we love the brethren" (I John 3:14). One of the ways to test yourself to see if you are in the faith (2 Corinthians 13:5) is to ask yourself if you have a love for other believers. If you have a love for other believers, then you will want to learn and grow with them by assembling together to worship the Lord and study His Word.

If the traditional structure of a pastor preaching to an audience within the confines of a church building does not appeal to you, know that there is a growing movement of home-based churches in the U.S. that allow for greater participation, interaction, and relationship building. You may want to find a house church in your area. Here are a few websites to help you find a house church in your area and to educate you on the biblical basis of the house church movement: www.house2house.tv, www.hccentral.com, www.openchurch.com. Whether you join a traditional church or a non-traditional church, the important thing is that you join a family of believers committed to the authority of the Bible and to helping each other grow in the faith. May God bless you as you begin your journey to a new life!

Contact Information

If you would like for Aaron D. Taylor to speak at your church or to conduct an evangelistic outreach in your community, you can contact him at fromdeathtolife@gmail.com

Aaron D. Taylor is the founder of a missionary organization called Great Commission Society. Great Commission Society is an organization dedicated to taking the gospel to those who have not yet heard. To find out more about Great Commission Society, go to www.greatcommissionsociety.com.

If you would like to help sponsor a native evangelist through Great Commission Society, please send your name and address to:

Great Commission Society
P.O. Box 400
Arnold, MO 63010

Endnotes

[1] Micah 6:8.

[2] Matthew 23:37.

[3] John 1:10.

[4] I Peter 1:20, Revelation 5:9.

[5] This is not to say that man is in any way equal with God. It simply means that man is of such quality of nature that he can communicate with God and reflect His glory. See Psalms 8:5 where the Psalmist says that man is a "little lower than the angels." The word for "angels" in this passage is *Elohim*. Elsewhere, it is a reference to God Himself. Some translations translate this word as "God" and not "angels."

[6] For proof that fallen angels were never given a second chance, see 2 Peter 2:4. While it is unclear if Lucifer and Satan are one and the same, it stands to reason that Satan was once an angelic being created with a free will.

[7] Hebrews 2:16 says, "For indeed He does not give aid to angels, but He does give aid to the seed of Abraham." The words used for "give aid to" in the original Greek mean "to take on the nature of." The writer of Hebrews also saw it as significant that God never took on the nature of an angel, but He did take on the nature of a man.

[8] Luke 22:42.

[9] Matthew 26:40.

[10] See Mark 14:50.

[11] Luke 23:34.

[12] I Timothy 5:6.

[13] Ecclesiastes 1:14.

[14] I John 4:19.

[15] Hebrews 4:15.

[16] Romans 5:8.

[17] John 15:12.

[18] I John 4:11.

[19] Romans 9:31-32.

[20] Galatians 2:21.

[21] Romans 3:23.

[22] Romans 14:9.

[23] John 12:23.

[24] Colossians 1:16.

[25] Compare Isaiah 6:1-3 with John 12:41. Notice how John identifies Jesus as the one whom the angels worshiped in Isaiah's vision.

[26] See Isaiah 14:12-14. This is the classic passage on the fall of Lucifer.

[27] When you put passages of Scripture together such as 2 Peter 2:4, Isaiah 14:12-14, Jude 1:6, Matthew 25:41,and Revelation 12:7-9, the idea that Satan's fallen angels were once heavenly angels becomes highly evident.

[28] Genesis 1:28.

[29] Genesis 1:26.

[30] See Ephesians 3:10.

[31] See 2 Corinthians 5:17.

[32] Ephesians 3:10.

[33] Ephesians 3:10-11.

[34] Ephesians 3:9.

[35] Ephesians 1:10.

[36] If you are wondering why I consistently emphasize that Jesus is "God the Son" when the Bible often refers to Jesus as the "Son of God," I do this to emphasize the eternal nature of His deity and sonship. If you read Hebrews 1:5-13, you will notice a conversation that took place before time began where God the Father talks with the Son. In the conversation, God (the Father) clearly calls the Son "God." This not only tells us that Jesus is God, it also tells us that Jesus, from eternity past, has always related to God the Father as the eternal Son. This is why

I refer to Jesus as God the Son. Another pre-incarnate term for Jesus is the "Word of God" (John 1:1). It is obvious in the Scriptures that the Word of God and the Son of God is the same person.

[37] Universal, that is, to those who believe. The benefits of Christ's sacrifice do not apply to unbelievers or to fallen angels. See Mark 16:16 and Matthew 25:41.

[38] I Corinthians 1:18-21.

[39] See Mathew 3:16-17, 28:19, 2 Corinthians 13:14, and I Peter 1:2 for examples of all three persons of the Godhead working together. For proof that the Holy Spirit is also God and not just an impersonal force, see Acts 5:3-4, I Corinthians 12:4-6, II Corinthians 3:17, and Ephesians 4:30.

[40] Mark 15:15.

[41] Genesis 1:28.

[42] The story of God scattering the peoples after the tower of Babel incident is found in Genesis 11:1-9.

[43] See Romans 1:20-32.

[44] For a detailed explanation of this concept, read Romans chapter 11.

[45] See Galatians 3:7-9, 7:14, and 7:29.

[46] See Ephesians 2:14-18.

[47] See the parable of the wicked vinedressers in Matthew 21:33-43 for proof that the Great Commission responsibility has been temporarily taken from the Jewish people and given to the Church. I say temporarily because Romans 11:29 indicates that the Jewish people will one day be given back the responsibility to fulfill their mandate to be a light to the nations. Some believe this will happen simultaneously with the Church age; others believe that God has to remove the Church from the earth before this can happen.

[48] I do not wish to imply that the angels take a passive role in watching the events that are played out on earth. The Bible teaches that angels are very active in the affairs of man, especially for believers. See Hebrews 1:14.

[49] Revelation 5:9-10.

[50] I Corinthians 15:24.

[51] Romans 11:36.

[52] Numbers 14:20-21.

[53] Habakkuk 2:14.

[54] For proof of this, read I Corinthians chapter 7.

[55] See I Corinthians 2:8.

[56] Ephesians 6:12.

[57] Luke 4:18.

[58] II Corinthians 12:10.

[59] See I Corinthians 4:11.

[60] II Corinthians 9:8.

[61] Acts 10:38.

[62] Colossians 2:9-10.

[63] See II Corinthians 4:6-7, Ephesians 4:24.

[64] Colossians 2:27.

[65] II Thessalonians 2:14.

[66] I Peter 1:12.

[67] Matthew 11:11.

[68] I Corinthians 15:45. This verse in no way denies the bodily resurrection of Jesus. It does, however, emphasize the spiritual nature of the resurrection and its saving significance.

[69] II Corinthians 5:17.

[70] I Peter 1:12.

[71] Romans 6:6.

[72] Ephesians 2:1-6.

[73] Ephesians 4:24.

[74] For example, James 1:2, I Peter 1:6.

[75] Psalm 34:1.

[76] Matthew 16:24.

[77] Job 1:10-11.

[78] Job 1:21.

[79] See Job 38-41.

[80] Deuteronomy 29:29.

[81] James 5:10-11.

[82] Job 42:10.

[83] Psalms 50:15.

[84] Psalms 34:19.

[85] Acts 9:9, I Thessalonians 3:3.

[86] II Thessalonians 3:2.

[87] See Philippians 1:19.

[88] Philippians 4:6.

[89] II Corinthians 12:9.

[90] Hebrews 12:1.

[91] Revelation 6:10.

[92] The Great Tribulation is the time period referred to in the Bible as a time of great judgment on earth. Assuming literal interpretations of prophecies in the books of Daniel and Revelation, many believe that this will be a literal seven-year judgment on the earth. Some say that the Great Tribulation is the second half of Daniel's 70th week prophesied in Daniel 9:27. In this case the Great Tribulation would only be three and a half years. There are differences of opinion whether the Church will be around during this time or not.

[93] Having said this, I would like to say that there are good role models among Christian celebrities.

[94] Excerpt from *Revolution in World Missions* by K.P. Yohannan. Used by permission of Gospel for Asia (www.gfa.org).

[95] I Timothy 6:17.

[96] James 2:5.

[97] This happened in the country of Guinea Bissau.

[98] I Corinthians 4:8.

[99] Revelation 3:17.

[100] Excerpt from *Revolution in World Missions* by K.P. Yohannan. Used by permission of Gospel for Asia (www.gfa.org).

[101] Hebrews 11:35-38.

[102] I Corinthians 7:31.

[103] I am referring to the extreme teaching that a person can expect a hundred-fold return from putting money in the offering bucket. There are some who teach that this woman gave expecting to receive something in return from the Lord. While it is true that the Bible teaches the principle of sowing and reaping in regard to finances (see II Corinthians 9:6-10), there is no mathematical formula to giving

and receiving. This woman would certainly not have been familiar with the Pauline concept of sowing and reaping in regard to finances.

[103] All the information in this paragraph comes from Howard Culbertson of the Southern Nazarene University. As of this writing, it was last updated on June 2, 2005. The URL for the website is http://home.snu.edu/~hculbert.fs/1040.htm.

[104] See I John 2:2.

[105] Ephesians 5:14.

[106] See I Timothy 6:7.

[107] The story of the tower of Babel is found in Genesis 11:1-9.

[108] For proof that the Church is the spiritual seed of Abraham, see Galatians 3:29.

[109] Matthew 28:19.

[110] This number is taken from Ralph Winter's article "The Unfinished Task."

[111] John 12:32.

[112] This number is also taken from Ralph Winter's article "The Unfinished Task."

[113] For Scriptures on the Day of the Lord, see Obadiah 15, Joel 2:31, Zephaniah 1:14-18, II Thessalonians 2:1-12, and II Peter 3:10.

[114] II Peter 3:9.

[115] Acts 2:40.

[116] I Corinthians 2:1-5.

[117] John 14:12.

[118] There are, of course, exceptions to this. I have a great deal of respect for ministries on television that use their resources to help the poor and to finance gospel ministry throughout the world.

[119] Matthew 28:19, Mark 16:15.

[120] This thinking is based off Genesis chapter 16, particularly verse 12 which says that Ishmael would be a "wild man" and that "his hand would be against every man." This verse should not be understood as a characterization of the Arab people for all time. Such an overly simplistic view fails to recognize that, through the cross, Christ has broken down all ethnic barriers and distinctions. See Galatians 3:28 and Colossians 3:11. Another verse that shatters this view is Acts 2:11. One of the languages spoken on the Day of Pentecost was Arabic.

[121] This is based off a faulty interpretation of Genesis 9:22-26. Many white supremacists used the "curse of Ham" to justify enslaving black people.

Apparently, they never read Galatians 3:13, which says that "Christ has redeemed us from the curse of the law, having become a curse for us." Given verses such as this and others such as Galatians 3:28 and Colossians 3:11, it is evident that all racism and prejudice is totally foreign to the Christian way of thinking.

[122] Ephesians 2:14.

[123] From the article "Forgotten Christians" in the May 24, 2004 issue of *American Conservative*. According to this article, this number is down from 20% in 1948. Most have fled due to civil war (as is the case in Lebanon), persecution from their own people, or as a result of the hardship of the Israeli occupation of the West Bank, East Jerusalem, and the Gaza Strip.

[124] John 13:35.

[125] Acts 1:7-8.

[126] Matthew 28:19.

[127] John 21:22.

[128] I Timothy 6:17.

[129] Genesis 12:1-3.

[130] I John 3:17-18.

[131] Matthew 9:37.

[132] Romans 10:14-15.

Printed in the United States
39038LVS00009B/154-177